The Rose Metal Press Field Guide to Writing

FLASH NONFICTION

Also in This Series

The Rose Metal Press Field Guide to Writing Flash Fiction:
Tips from Editors, Teachers, and Writers in the Field
Edited by Tara L. Masih

The Rose Metal Press Field Guide to Prose Poetry:
Contemporary Poets in Discussion and Practice
Edited by Gary L. McDowell and F. Daniel Rzicznek

THE ROSE METAL PRESS

Field Guide to Writing

Flash Nonfiction

**Advice and Essential Exercises
from Respected Writers, Editors,
and Teachers**

Edited by Dinty W. Moore

Rose Metal Press

2012

Acknowledgments for previously published works appear on page 174, which constitutes an extension of the copyright page.

Rose Metal Press, Inc.
P.O. Box 1956
Brookline, MA 02446
rosemetalpress@gmail.com
www.rosemetalpress.com

Library of Congress Control Number: 2012913250

ISBN: 978-0-9846166-6-4

Cover and interior design by Rebecca Saraceno
Cover typefaces: Avenir and Utopia; Interior typefaces: Utopia, with Avenir
See "A Note About the Type" for more information about the type.

This book is manufactured in the United States of America and printed on acid-free paper.

For Judith Kitchen, friend and inspiration

TABLE OF CONTENTS

Mapping the Terrain: A Preface IX

INTRODUCTION
XIII – Of Fire and Ice: The Pleasing Sting of Flash Nonfiction – *Dinty W. Moore*

MYSTERIOUS, AMBITIOUS, AND INTIMATE: THE FLASH NONFICTION FORM
1 – On Miniatures – *Lia Purpura*

8 – Writing into the Flash: On Finding Short Nonfiction's Decisive Moment – *Barrie Jean Borich*

15 – On Carnival Lights, Compression, and Mice – *Carol Guess*

22 – Writing in Place – *Bret Lott*

"NO IDEAS BUT IN THINGS": THE POWER OF IMAGE AND DETAIL
28 – Friendship, Intuition, and Trust: On the Importance of Detail – *Brenda Miller*

33 – Memory Triggers and Tropes – *Rigoberto González*

37 – Paper Clips, Sausage, Candy Cigarettes, Silk: "Thingy-ness" in Flash Nonfiction – *Anne Panning*

43 – The Ant in the Water Droplet – *Philip Graham*

50 – The Wound of the Photograph: A Meditation on the Well-Chosen Detail – *Robin Hemley*

SPEAKING TO THE READER: ON FINDING YOUR VOICE
57 – Crafting Voice – *Jennifer Sinor*

64 – Communal and Personal Voices – *Lee Martin*

70 – Writing Though Innocence and Experience: Voices in Flash Nonfiction – *Sue William Silverman*

WORDS, WONDERFUL WORDS: USING SOUND AND LANGUAGE

76 – The Sounds and Sense of Sentences – *Barbara Hurd*

82 – Location, Location, Location – *Peggy Shumaker*

86 – Word Hoards: On Diction and the Riches of the English Language – *Eric LeMay*

OF YOU AND I: THOUGHTS ON POINT-OF-VIEW

93 – Bye-Bye, I, and Hello, You – *Ira Sukrungruang*

100 – All About You – *Dinah Lenney*

105 – Weaving Past, Present, and Future in Flash Nonfiction – *Norma Elia Cantú*

SETTLING ON STRUCTURE: SHAPING FLASH NONFICTION

113 – Over the River and Through the Woods, to Almanac We Go: On the Use of Research and Lists in Flash Nonfiction – *Aimee Nezhukumatathil*

118 – The Art of Digression – *Judith Kitchen*

126 – Building a Frame, Giving an Essay a Form – *Maggie McKnight*

THE SINGULAR MOMENT: WHERE TO BEGIN, WHERE TO END

134 – The Question of Where We Begin – *Kyle Minor*

142 – Of Artifacts and MRIs, or Stuck on the Web with You – *Nicole Walker*

151 – On Beginnings and Endings – *Jenny Boully*

AGAINST THE GRAIN: ALTERNATIVE APPROACHES TO FLASH NONFICTION

157 – Writing the Brief Contrary Essay – *Patrick Madden*

164 – Walking, Gathering, Listening: Writing from the Green World – *Jeff Gundy*

Further Reading 171

Credits 174

Acknowledgments 176

About the Editor 178

A Note About the Type 179

MAPPING THE TERRAIN
A Preface

In January 2010, Dinty W. Moore sent us an email proposing a third book in our popular *Field Guide* series, *The Rose Metal Press Field Guide to Writing Flash Nonfiction,* which would focus on "composing excellent memoir, essay, and factual writing in the very short form."

The timing was perfect. We had recently been discussing two goals we had for Rose Metal: first, to broaden the scope of our list by soliciting more work in hybrid nonfiction forms, and second, to develop our *Field Guide* series into a trilogy—a trifecta of craft study of hybrid forms. Dinty's proposed book was exactly what we had been hoping for and hadn't yet articulated.

We were also excited by the opportunity to work with Dinty again. He had long been a friend of the Press: reading and blurbing an early manuscript of *The Rose Metal Press Field Guide to Writing Flash Fiction,* and judging our Fourth Annual Short Short Chapbook Contest. Meanwhile, we had long been admirers of his writing and his work on the journal *Brevity,* which has done so much to bring attention to the short nonfiction form. Started by Dinty in 1997, *Brevity: A Journal of Concise Literary Nonfiction* has been the online face and voice of flash nonfiction, publishing primarily creative essays of 750 words or less by both the genre's newest and most established writers, as well as craft essays, book reviews, and a blog.

Dinty also possessed the exact triad of skills that we aim to embody in each *Field Guide*: the perspectives of writers, teachers, and editors. Dinty's career and qualifications attest to his ability to shift seamlessly among all three viewpoints: he has written extensively in and about the nonfiction form, he has taught nonfiction at various universities, and he has edited a number of anthologies and *Brevity*. He would have no trouble assembling a group of respected essayists for *The Rose Metal Press Field Guide to Writing Flash Nonfiction* that represented all of those perspectives and more, offering the first book-length discussion of the craft of writing flash nonfiction.

As with our previous *Field Guides*, we didn't want to weigh down or pigeon-hole flash nonfiction with strict definitions, word counts, or jargon-laden scholarly analysis. Encompassing any number of sub-genres and possibilities—memoir, argumentative, informative, personal, braided, mosaic, and meditative essays, to name just a few—flash nonfiction seemed our slipperiest genre yet. How to go about creating a cohesive craft guide without limiting the form with arbitrary parameters and labels?

Luckily Dinty had a solution, right there in the second paragraph of his pitch letter:

> In his introduction to the anthology *In Short*, Bernard Cooper suggests that short nonfiction requires "an alertness to detail, a quickening of the senses, a focusing of the literary lens ... until one has magnified some small aspect of what it means to be human." This captures the challenge very well, I think, and the *Field Guide* will attempt to break down the units of his recipe—alertness, quickening, focus—into understandable craft elements.

Some small aspect of what it means to be human—a binding force full of craft essay possibilities. Also a tall order, but one that gets at the heart of what's so compelling about good flash nonfiction: the writer's experience of the world made small and large at the same time. While flash fiction has been getting the majority of the short form publicity in recent years, this sister species of flash has been steadily growing more popular among readers and writers. Bound by similar length restrictions as flash fiction, short form nonfiction also contends with another major challenge: the constraint of telling the truth. The writer's life and thoughts are compressed and placed on the page to be examined by the reader with neither extended exposition nor the veil of fiction for protection.

The *Field Guide* that follows is everything we hoped for when we enthusiastically read Dinty's pitch two and a half years ago. As a press devoted to bringing literary attention and readership to hard-to-categorize and under-appreciated genres, we are proud to offer a book that illuminates flash nonfiction with a diverse range of views and voices, as well as with wisdom, humor, and compelling prose. Being human has many aspects, so you may find yourself laughing at a witty discussion of point of view, wondering at the smallest details of the animal world laid bare, gasping as dogs and children put themselves in danger, and grieving over essay examples about September 11th and Hurricane Katrina. Throughout this book many small aspects of what it means to be a writer, editor, and teacher of flash nonfiction form a multi-dimensional discourse on a beloved and burgeoning genre.

Dinty's **introduction** offers a detailed history of the form, following the genre from early Classical manifestations in Greece and Japan, through the influence of French father of the essay Michel de Montaigne and the essay's evolution in England and the U.S. as printing technologies made it more widely available, to the coalescence of a more defined flash nonfiction form in the 1980s and 1990s and the genre's amazing popularity today.

Twenty-six conversational, insightful essays follow, all written by current practitioners, editors, and teachers of the form, and each illuminating a different aspect of the craft of writing flash nonfiction. Each essay ends with an **exercise** or **prompt**, as well as an **essay example** so that readers can test out and apply the ideas of the essayists to their own writing and study. The table of contents groups the essays by subject, which helps direct readers and teachers to areas of particular interest. These essays, exercises, and examples make great teaching tools, both in the classroom and for individual study, but are also meant to be an enjoyable and thought-provoking read for anyone interested in the genre and its various voices, traditions, and manifestations.

Like the previous *Field Guides*, this one concludes with a **list of further reading** in flash nonfiction, suggested by the press, editors, and essayists, and showcasing the richness and diversity of the field.

In this third *Field Guide* installment, we were also thrilled to once again have at our disposal the amazing skill of book designer Rebecca Saraceno, and a beautiful new piece of crow cover art from Pamela Callahan. Pamela's crows, in their many poses and articulations, have become the emblem of our *Field Guide* series, representing our goal of taking the concept of a field guide and its cataloging of the flora and fauna of a region for those exploring it, and making the format exciting and new, yet recognizable, by applying it to genres that have yet to be taken stock of and examined. Pamela's crows gather, blend, shadow, swim, play, and defy expectations.

We hope this *Field Guide* will encourage you to engage more fully with the startling and wonderfully hybrid landscape of flash nonfiction. As with all great nonfiction, it's your own experience that matters, distilled down to those instants of image and truth worth sharing that you find along the trail.

—*Abigail Beckel & Kathleen Rooney*
Rose Metal Press, 2012

OF FIRE AND ICE
The Pleasing Sting of Flash Nonfiction

Searching for early references to the flash nonfiction form eventually led me to William Makepeace Thackeray's *Roundabout Papers* and the term "essaykin." Thackeray, in his 1863 collection of essays and magazine pieces, describes a parlor game where an anecdote is recited to everyone in the room. After the anecdote is shared, each guest "writes down, to the best of his memory and ability, the anecdote just narrated." Then, each person in the room takes a turn reading their versions aloud. The fun of the game, Thackeray reports, is that the "original story becomes so changed and distorted that at the end of all the statements you are puzzled to know where the truth is at all."

Of his own anecdotal contributions, Thackeray adds: "In these humble essaykins, I have taken leave to egotize."

Thackeray's account is amusing, and remarkably enough seems to bear the early seeds of those current controversies surrounding the creative nonfiction genre: the subjectivity of truth, the vagaries of memory, and the risk of "navel-gazing" in memoir. His term essaykin, however, never caught on.

In fact, no single term has ever truly taken hold to represent the myriad ways in which authors over the centuries have embraced the very short form of thoughtful, artful nonfiction. For the most part, all nonfiction aimed at literary readers has been lumped together under one umbrella, no matter what the length. The earliest writings of Greek and Roman philosophers, the brief *essais* of Michel de Montaigne, Ben Franklin's celebrated aphorisms, the shorter journalistic pieces of Mark Twain, and contributors to *The New Yorker*'s "Talk of the Town" section have continued a tradition that has remained unstudied and, until very recently, unlabeled. Some works were long, some were short, some were very short, but little was done to form any theoretical understanding of how the "flash" form works, and what was possible in the small space of a page or two.

This lack of study or discussion is precisely the gap I seek to address here, with *The Rose Metal Press Field Guide to Writing Flash Nonfiction: Advice and Essential Exercises from Respected Writers, Editors, and Teachers.* Assisted by the 26 talented contributors represented in this anthology, plus a few extra and outstanding authors featured in the example essays provided, I hope to extend the conversation begun by Judith Kitchen and Mary Paumier Jones in 1996 when they published *In Short,* the first of their three excellent anthologies of brief contemporary creative nonfiction.

First however, it is important to define what I mean by brief and also what I mean by literary or creative nonfiction, since the overlap with other forms of nonfiction is considerable.

For the purposes of my historical analysis below, I am including creative nonfiction work up to 2,000 words, though the great majority of what is discussed is briefer: 500 to 1,000 words, and sometimes even fewer. While newspaper articles, editorials and editorial columns, sermons, brief informational articles in magazines, and even college composition essays, all fall within the brief word-count range, they are, for the most part, not included or discussed here. Literary nonfiction is not merely informational or topical, and it is not primarily intended to be persuasive. Instead, like literary fiction and poetry, the nonfiction we discuss is marked by the distinct, often peculiar, voice and sensibilities of the author and these works examine the deeply human—and often unanswerable—questions that concern all serious art. The style might range from intellectual to somber to humorous to playful, and the subject matter might be travel, the inscrutability of human behavior, or a moth on a window ledge, but the work itself is individual, intimate, exploratory, and carefully crafted using metaphor, sensory language, and precise detail.

As you follow my abbreviated historical timeline, you will see how brief nonfiction (and literary nonfiction generally) gradually transforms from work primarily focused on ideas, values, and political issues to a preponderance of memoir, an exploration of the self and the meanings of our individual lives. Over time, the medium of delivery—oration, transcription, early printing technology, advances in publishing and distribution (and wider literacy), and eventually digital technologies—has impacted the nature of the work, its length, and its presentation. But all along the way, brief nonfiction has attempted to capture the reader's attention and imagination in the first few words, and to hold it—uninterrupted—until the final period.

The Origins of the Brief Essay

The genesis of the short essay goes further back than Thackeray's game, certainly. One might credibly place the beginning of the brief form with the early Greek philosopher Heraclitus, whose aphoristic meditations on human nature and politics date back to roughly 500 B.C. The Roman author Seneca wrote a series of letters from exile, often translated as *Moral Epistles*, around 60 A.D., and these shorter works have also been cited by later essayists as a significant influence.

In his important history of the essay form, *The Art of the Personal Essay: An Anthology from the Classical Era to the Present* (1997), Phillip Lopate also cites the Greek historian Plutarch, and the Japanese writer Sei Shōnagon, whose *The Pillow Book*—an 11th-century collection of court observations, gossip, poetry, and lists—is not only an early example of the short essay but also one of the first known works by a female essayist. Lopate additionally points to a second Japanese writer, Kenkō, who penned brief items translated under the title, *Essays in Idleness*, in the early 14th century.

Michel de Montaigne, a highly-educated French nobleman who retired from public duties and retreated to his family's castle around 1570 to focus on his writing, is often called the father of the essay, and he is certainly an important touchstone as we explore the briefer form. In his 20 or so years of devoted authorship, he produced more than a thousand pages of wide-ranging observation that he called "*essais*," or "attempts." While some of his longer essays—for instance "Of Presumption" and "Upon Some Verses of Virgil"—range from 12,000 to 20,000 words, he also penned a number of very brief works, including "Of Age," a 1,000-word meditation on lifespan, and the playful "Of Thumbs," which comes in at just over 300 words.

For the most part, Montaigne's essays are idiosyncratic attempts to explore complex questions, both personal and philosophical. Among his revolutionary ideas was that he needn't speak for all mankind, but could illuminate and extend knowledge through an honest, painstaking exploration of *one* man, himself. As he wrote in "Of Repentance":

> Others form man; I only report him: and represent a particular
> one, ill fashioned enough, and whom, if I had to model him
> anew, I should certainly make something else than what he is
> … I cannot fix my object; 'tis always tottering and reeling by a
> natural giddiness: I take it as it is at the instant I consider it; I do
> not paint its being, I paint its passage; not a passing from one
> age to another, or, as the people say, from seven to seven years,
> but from day to day, from minute to minute.

Montaigne's highly individual "movement of the mind" style—tracking his thoughts on the page to create a compelling narrative of inquiry—shapes the essay form, and all of literary nonfiction, to this day.

Many of the early British practitioners of the essay form—including, for instance, Francis Bacon, Joseph Addison, Richard Steele, and Margaret Cavendish—grew directly out of the Montaignean tradition. Bacon definitely favored the shorter form, perhaps because he was more definitive than his French predecessor. In his collection, *Essays or Counsels, Civil and Moral* (1625), Bacon offers up 58 concise nonfiction pieces, offering his views on religion, child-rearing, human relationships, education, and virtue. In 1711, Addison and Steele, themselves noted essayists, joined forces to found a magazine known as *The Spectator,* a daily publication of breezy, conversational essays, most of them quite brief. Other important works by British essayists of the time include Charles Lamb's *Essays of Elia* (1823) and William Hazlitt's *The Plain Speaker: Opinions on Books, Men, and Things* (1826).

By the end of the 19th century, the essay was flourishing and already evolving in numerous directions, earning its reputation as the most flexible of forms.

The Brief Essay in America

Benjamin Franklin, one might argue, was the first brief literary essayist on American soil, if you count the concise entries on weather and
astrological events and the advice on etiquette he inserted into his *Poor
Richard's Almanack*, an annual publication he inaugurated in 1733. You
can certainly hear the faint echo of Montaigne's cantankerous humor
in Franklin's suggestions such as "Fish and visitors stink in three days."

The 1800s were full of brief prose, thanks to the proliferation of
newspapers and magazines and rapidly advancing printing technologies, but the rather loose separation between true stories, fictionalized
accounts, tall tales, "yellow journalism," and instructive fables makes it
somewhat difficult to pinpoint what falls clearly into the literary nonfiction category.

Like his contemporary across the ocean Charles Dickens, the American author Washington Irving was primarily known for his fiction, but
also penned numerous short character "sketches," some obviously fabulous and imagined, others closer to the truth. Many of these appeared in
The Sketch Book of Geoffrey Crayon, Gent., also known as just *The Sketch
Book* (1820).

Fanny Fern, the pen name of Sara Payson Willis, was a widely read
columnist of the time, and her collected short works, *Fern Leaves* (1853),
was a best-seller. Here is an excerpt from her very brief essay "The Best of
Men Have Their Failings," exhibiting her wry, sarcastic outlook on mid-
century morals:

> ... I've always warped to the opinion that good men were as safe
> as homeopathic pills. You don't suppose they ever patronize false
> words or false weights, false measures or false yardsticks? ... You
> don't suppose they ever bestow a charity to have it trumpeted in
> the newspapers? You don't suppose, when they trot devoutly to
> meeting twice a day on Sunday that they overhaul their ledgers
> in the intermission? You don't suppose they ever put doubtful-
> looking bank bills in the contribution box? You don't suppose
> they ever pay their minister's salary in consumptive hens and
> damaged turkeys? I wish people were not so uncharitable and
> suspicious. It disgusts me with human nature.

Another early American essay writer worthy of mention here is Henry David Thoreau, best known for his nonfiction account, *Walden; or, Life in the Woods* (1854). Though collected in book form, many of the chapters from *Walden*, and from later books, including *The Maine Woods* (1864), read like stand-alone essays, some falling into the briefer range. Whatever his intention, he is often-excerpted and anthologized in the briefer form, and his work remains an important source for today's environmental essayists.

Novelist Mark Twain (born Samuel Langhorne Clemens) is especially problematic in tracing the brief essay form. Though I said earlier in this introduction that I would by-and-large make a distinction between newspaper articles and more literary forms of nonfiction, Twain's travel pieces written for various newspapers, and later collected in books such as *The Innocents Abroad or The New Pilgrims' Progress* (1869) and *Roughing It* (1872), were so marked by his strong voice and individual style that he clearly falls into the literary tradition. The second problem with Twain, however, is that by his own admission he mixed fact and fiction freely, especially in service of humor. His publishers didn't seem to care, either, as long as newspapers and books flew off the shelves.

Zora Neale Hurston, author of the novel *Their Eyes Were Watching God* (1937) and an important figure in the Harlem Renaissance, was also an essayist. Her widely read and often-anthologized 1928 essay "How It Feels to Be Colored Me" comes in at just over 1,500 words.

As reading, and magazine sales, grew rapidly into the early 20th century, the list of writers employing the brief literary nonfiction form grew as well. Certainly many of the magazine writers who were part of the legendary Algonquin Round Table, the irreverent and celebrated luncheon of New York City critics, playwrights, and humorists that continued each weekday for nearly a decade, such as Robert Benchley, Dorothy Parker, and Heywood Broun, should be included. Also at the table, of course, was Harold Ross, who founded *The New Yorker* in 1925, and Alexander Woollcott, who instituted the magazine's "Shouts and Murmurs" page a few years later.

Noted authors James Thurber, S. J. Perelman, and E. B. White also wrote a miscellany of brief pieces for *The New Yorker*. Though often viewed as light or "occasional" pieces, the very short nonfiction that has been featured throughout *The New Yorker's* pages over the past 87 years includes many memorable short works, especially important in the way that they have merged conventional journalism and sophisticated literary style.

Many of those we consider to be the most important American essayists of the mid-20th century, including for instance James Baldwin, Mary McCarthy, and Edward Hoagland, wrote at various lengths, and for a wide variety of magazines and journals. None of them could especially be said to have focused on the short form, however. That would have to wait until the final few decades of the 1900s.

The Contemporary Brief Essay

To understand changes in the brief nonfiction form in the latter half of the 20th century, it is important to note the energy and activity that coalesced around the brief *fiction* genre. Important anthologies such as *Sudden Fiction: American Short-Short Stories (1983)*, *Flash Fiction: 72 Very Short Stories (1992)*, and *Micro Fiction: An Anthology of Fifty Really Short Stories (1996)*, not only drew attention to the growing canon of short short stories, but also attempted to give the work a proper name. The term "flash" became the most widely used term and remains the standard to this day.

The flash fiction movement spawned by these anthologies led to a greater acceptance of these shorter prose works in literary magazines, and this in turn created more opportunities for flash *non*fiction. This era, the 1980s through the 1990s, also marked the first use of the now common term "creative nonfiction" and the rapid turn toward work that was more memoir-based as opposed to purely essayistic or journalistic.

The next important step forward came from editors Judith Kitchen and Mary Paumier Jones, who published the first of three fine brief nonfiction anthologies, *In Short*, in 1996. Kitchen credits her co-editor with the original idea to collect essays "in these smaller increments," which the two chose to define as 2,000 words or fewer.

Why 2,000 words?

"We knew that short pieces can tend to get longer and longer, so we wanted room for flexibility," Kitchen has explained, "but not too much.

The actual 2,000 mark was purely arbitrary— but in the end, it worked for us."

Introducing the collection—which proved so popular that it was followed by a second, *In Brief (1999)*, and a third, *Short Takes (2005)*—Bernard Cooper offers perhaps the first attempt to define the brief essay form. He begins his analysis with the visual arts, remembering an early attraction to Joseph Cornell's celebrated assemblages, odd groupings of found objects contained by the four sides of a wooden box.

"Cornell's assemblages are willfully insular and fragmentary," Cooper writes. "Yet the containment of his art is the very source of its drama, in much the same way haiku is made all the more acute by its brevity." Cooper also reminisces on the packets of miniature human figures sold for use in model train landscapes. "At arm's length the people look like plastic slivers," Cooper writes:

> Only when you bring the boxes close can you begin to make out
> the cut of a jacket, the length of a skirt, and closer still—though
> you have to squint in speculation—the expression on a face...
> I find this Lilliputian populace to be every bit as wistful and
> evocative as the wide sky on a starry night; holding the boxes up
> to the light reminds me anew how small we are, how alone in our
> separate compartments, how elusive our traits to the naked eye.

To paraphrase Cooper, then, the brief essay form is discrete, sharply focused, and must be held up, studied like a small tableau, to reveal the secrets of human nature contained therein.

Cooper, in his nonfiction collection *Maps to Anywhere (1997)*, was among the handful of contemporary authors who in the 1980s and 1990s began a deliberate experimentation with very short essays. Others include William Least Heat Moon (*Blue Highways*, 1989), Eduardo Galeano (*The Book of Embraces*, 1992), Michael Ondaatje (*Running in the Family*, 1993), Abigail Thomas (*Safekeeping*, 2001), and Naomi Shihab Nye (*Mint Snowball*, 2001). These brief pieces sometimes appeared in small literary magazines, in some cases as "prose poems," since the terms "brief essay" or "flash nonfiction" had not yet gained wide acceptance.

In 1997, I started the online journal *Brevity*, which upped (or downed) the ante set by Kitchen and Paumier Jones from 2,000 words to 750 words or fewer. My inspiration for *Brevity* came partly from Kitchen's anthology, and partly from my interest in the flash fiction form. My choice of 750 words as compared to the 2,000 words allowed by Kitchen and Paumier Jones reflected both the limits set by the short short fiction anthologies—*Sudden Fiction* allowed up to 1,750 words, roughly, while *Flash Fiction* made a point of bringing that limit lower, to near the 750 word mark—and also my sense that shorter works would be more agreeable to a reader encountering the work on a computer screen.

This tendency toward briefer prose in the digital domain stems partially from the eyestrain caused by staring too long into a conventional computer monitor and also from the perceived unwillingness of computer surfers to scroll too far or too often. The advent of blogs, Facebook, Tumblrs, and Twitter seems to validate the idea that shorter chunks of prose are more enticing to users of these new technologies. Not everyone, of course, agrees as to whether this is a good thing, a bad thing, or simply the way media and information changes over time.

Brevity has grown beyond my wildest expectations in its 16 years of existence, and, judging from the ever-multiplying numbers of submissions and the geographic locales of those who submit, the flash nonfiction movement has flourished in tandem with the online magazine.

One other significant influence on the brief nonfiction form was the *Seneca Review*, particularly the fall 1997 issue in which editors Deborah Tall and John D'Agata recognized a growing canon of creative nonfiction that "straddles the essay and the lyric poem ... forsak(ing) narrative line, discursive logic, and the art of persuasion in favor of idiosyncratic meditation." The "lyric essay," as it has come to be called, does not always require extreme brevity, but quite often it falls within the shorter range.

The 1997 issue included brief prose works by Anne Carson, David Shields, Joe Wenderoth, and Terry Tempest Williams, and subsequent issues have included Russell Edson, Denis Johnson, and more than a few of the authors represented in this *Rose Metal Press Field Guide*. Like the prose poem, the lyric essay defies strict definition, but—when in the realm of nonfiction—both forms overlap the brief essay in numerous ways, not the least of which include their tightly packed language, their quick scenes, and their concise imagery.

These factors—the explosion of interest in flash fiction, the *In Short* anthology of brief nonfiction, and, I like to think, the presence of *Brevity,* the first magazine devoted solely to the brief essay—paved the way for flash nonfiction to become a genre of its own, with a wide readership and numerous publication venues.

While a few additional journals featuring flash nonfiction have arrived over the years, including *Blip, DIAGRAM, Hippocampus, Flashquake,* and *Sweet: A Literary Confection,* perhaps the most important development is that flash is seen regularly in conventional literary journals, those that include longer form prose and poetry, and this includes both online journals and conventional paper and ink magazines. Community writing centers now offer courses in "writing the brief essay," and numerous college nonfiction workshops now focus part or all of a semester on investigating this short form. *Creative Nonfiction* magazine runs an ongoing "#cnftweet" competition, entitled "Tiny Truths," which asks for work that is no more than 130 characters.

As the computer screen grows even smaller with the rapid proliferation of tablets and smart phones, I can only guess at what is on the horizon, but to paraphrase William Shakespeare, "Brevity may very well be the soul of our literary future."

Toward a Definition

As editor of *Brevity,* I am often asked to define and demarcate the flash nonfiction genre. Many will initially assume a flash piece is an excerpt from a longer work, and yes, sometimes a significant moment out of a chapter or a long essay can stand alone, but the best flash work in my opinion could never work in the longer form because the energy of the piece hinges on the rapid-fire sharing of information. The urgency of having to fit the content into an abbreviated frame is what makes it powerful.

Though trying to pin down any art form too strictly is ultimately a fruitless exercise, I've come up with what I think is an apt metaphor: Imagine there is a fire burning deep in the forest. In an essay of conventional length, the reader begins at the forest's edge, and is taken on a hike, perhaps a meandering stroll, into those woods, in search of that fire. The further in the reader goes, with each page that turns, the more the reader begins to sense smoke in the air, or maybe heat, or just an awareness that something ahead is smoldering.

In a very brief essay, however, the reader is not a hiker but a smoke jumper, one of those brave firefighters who jump out of planes and land 30 yards from where the forest fire is burning. The writer starts the reader right at that spot, at the edge of the fire, or as close as one can get without touching the actual flame. There is no time to walk in.

The brief essay, in other words, needs to be hot from the first sentence, and the heat must remain the entire time. My fire metaphor, it is important to note, does not refer to incendiary subject matter. The heat might come from language, from image, from voice or point-of-view, from revelation or suspense, but there must always be a burning urgency of some sort, translated through each sentence, starting with the first.

Judith Kitchen has her own comparison, focusing on ice instead of fire. "I often use a snowball metaphor," she has said. "You've got all this stuff out there called snow but when you gather it all up and really pack it together, you know, and you throw it off, there's a sting. I think with these short pieces—even when they're quiet and meditative—the effect is a little sting."

Fire or ice?

Either way, the air changes.

The *Field Guide*

This book, *The Rose Metal Press Field Guide to Writing Flash Nonfiction*, offers additional definitions of the genre, from respected teachers, editors, and practitioners. But of course, literary writing is an art form, and no one definition can ever successfully pin down artistic production or product. Still, you'll find remarkable agreement here on the basic components of the shorter form.

Each of the craft essays, writing prompts, and example essays that follow attempt to identify, isolate, and illuminate the "best practices" common to contemporary nonfiction flash. Some components are truly unique—for instance, the extreme concision—while others—voice, point-of-view, structure—are familiar from other forms of literary nonfiction but often function differently in shorter pieces.

Lia Purpura sets the table with her absorbing reflection on why we are attracted to all things miniature, from bonsai trees to tadpoles, miniature railroads to an infant's fingers and toes. She is joined in the opening portion of the conversation by Barrie Jean Borich, Carol Guess, and Bret Lott, who each in their own important way reflect on why the flash form exists and continues to fascinate.

Brenda Miller, Rigoberto González, Anne Panning, Philip Graham, and Robin Hemley offer different ways of understanding image and detail, or "thingy-ness," in flash nonfiction, while Jennifer Sinor, Lee Martin, and Sue William Silverman dissect the always-crucial question of how and where a writer finds her genuine voice.

As writers, we have many arrows in our quiver, or tools in our toolbox, but in the end, it all comes down to the words, both their meanings and sounds. Barbara Hurd, Peggy Shumaker, and Eric LeMay weigh in with examinations of the various rhythms, echoes, textures, and sonic pleasures of language.

Point-of-view includes not just the usual "first," "second," and "third person" approaches, but what a narrator knows, comprehends, and where he stands emotionally. Point-of-view can also involve something as basic as verb tense: are you looking at the past, discussing something current, or looking forward? Ira Sukrungruang, Dinah Lenney, and Norma Elia Cantú reveal how important it is to have control over this crucial element of flash prose.

Aimee Nezhukumatathil, Judith Kitchen, and Maggie McKnight examine how all of these building blocks of flash nonfiction—the urgency and immediacy, the "thingyness," voice and point-of-view, and the language itself—must exist within a structure, perhaps a simple or complex prose form, or a meandering river of thought, or even a graphic frame.

The question of structure, of course, begs one of the most crucial questions any flash writer must answer: where does it begin, and where does it end? With so few words available, Kyle Minor, Nicole Walker, and

Jenny Boully remind us, not one can be wasted on an initial clearing of the throat or a concluding ramble.

And finally, Patrick Madden harkens back to the essay's roots, with his call for more contrariness in the brief essay, and Jeff Gundy takes us back out into the world, "to chase squirrels and sniff around in the leaves," where we might quiet ourselves long enough to listen.

My hope is that you enjoy this book and learn from it, but most of all my hope is that you'll be inspired to write, revise, and write some more. And then keep writing.

—*Dinty W. Moore*

Editor

Athens, Ohio, 2012

The Rose Metal Press Field Guide to Writing

FLASH NONFICTION

Lia Purpura

ON MINIATURES

Why are miniature things so compelling?

First off, I don't mean the cute or the precious, those debased and easily dismissed forms of the miniature whose size compels our pity or protection; I mean workable things on very small scales. I'd like to offer some thoughts on shortness in prose by looking at miniatures in different forms and coming up with some characteristics that define them.

The miniature is mysterious. We wonder how all those parts work when they're so small. We wonder "are they real?" (A question never asked, of course, of giant things which are all too real.) It's why we linger over an infant's fingers and toes, those astonishing replicas: we can't quite *believe* they work. Chihuahuas work. Birds and bonsai trees work. Girl gymnasts work. Miniatures are the familiar, reduced to unfamiliarity. Miniatures are improbable, unlikely. Causes to marvel. Surprises. Feats of engineering. Products of an obsessive detailer.

Miniatures offer changes of scale by which we measure ourselves anew. On one hand, miniatures posit an omniscient onlooker, able to take in the whole at once. Consider your *self* in relation to dollhouses, snow globes, Fabergé eggs, sugar Easter eggs with sugary scenes inside, reliquaries, flies in amber, frog spawn, terrariums, aquariums, souvenir key chains you look through to see a picture of the very spot you're visiting,

Lia Purpura's books include *On Looking* (2006), a finalist for the National Book Critics Circle Award, *King Baby* (2008), winner of the Beatrice Hawley Award, and a new collection of essays, *Rough Likeness* (2012). Her awards include a 2012 Guggenheim Fellowship, the AWP Award in Nonfiction, the Ohio State University Press Award in Poetry, and NEA and Fulbright Fellowships. Recent work has appeared in *Agni, Orion, The New Republic, The New Yorker,* and *Best American Essays*. She lives in Baltimore, where she is writer in residence at Loyola University, and also teaches in the Rainier Writing Workshop MFA Program.

stilled. You are large enough to hold such things fully in hand. You obtain all the space around it. On the other hand, miniatures compel us to transcend spatial norms, issue invitations to their realm, and suggest we forget or disregard our size. In dollhouse land, you can walk through the kitchen, living room, bedroom with your three-inch-high friend, and, face pressed to the window, feel the cushions of the thumbnail loveseat hold you. In the presence of miniatures we can renounce our sense of omniscience. And in this realm, fit inside the miniature, we experience certain states of being or belief: worlds in a grain of sand; eternities in wildflowers. Regions beyond our normal-sized perception. Whether we are, in relation to them, omniscient or companionably small beings, miniatures invite us to leave our known selves and perspectives behind.

The miniature is unto itself, not a mere part of a whole, like a fetish or an excerpt. Certainly smaller, component parts make up an epic—I'm thinking of paintings like Bosch's *Garden of Earthly Delights*; Bruegel's *Childrens' Games*, and of Alexander Calder's *Circus*—in which all the individual parts are certainly compelling. But the miniature begins and ends in itself. One rank, Boschian egg-shaped, half-human/half-bird hacking another with a sword is thrilling, but it is not a whole painting unto itself. It's a snippet.

Miniatures are ambitious. Charles Simic once called Franz Wright "a miniaturist whose secret ambition is to write an epic on the inside of a matchbook cover." When you pair the words "ambition" and "matchbook cover" a tension develops. Gaston Bachelard notes in *The Poetics of Space* that "when descriptions tell things in tiny detail, they are automatically verbose." In other words, in a miniature, everything is significant. Everything "counts." In her book *On Longing*, Susan Stewart uses the example of a miniature railroad to show the relationship between a reduction of scale and a corresponding increase in detail and significance. I recently saw a particularly outrageous example of this "increase in detail": a Fabergé egg, commemorating the Trans-Siberian Railway, which contained a seven-car train—and indeed it was the *detail* that fascinated. The headlights were diamonds, the taillights were rubies, great pains were taken with other jewels, and all was set in motion with a pea-sized golden key. I could imagine a little czarina kept busy for hours unloading boxcars full of jeweled fruit.

Miniatures are practical. Like mementos they can be carried out of a burning house or by immigrants to the New World; they can be held under the tongue like contraband and smuggled past border guards. Miniatures are made to travel. They are portable and light, dense and compressed as diamonds. Italo Calvino chose to call his Charles Eliot Norton Lectures *Six Memos for the Next Millennium.* In the introductory note to the collection, his wife writes that Calvino was "delighted by the word 'memos' and dismissed grander titles such as 'Some Literary Values' and 'Six Literary Legacies'." Instead he titled his memos "lightness," "quickness," "exactitude," "visibility," "multiplicity," and "consistency." The whole book is only 120 pages or so long. And while I'm recommending, there's Lawrence Sutin's *A Postcard Memoir,* a collection of essays, each of which is made to fit on a postcard, and each sketching out in part an era in the author's life and family's history. Such brevity "serves as a refuge for greatness" or brevity gives greatness (the historical, the philosophical) a practical form in which to travel.

Miniatures encourage attention—in the way whispering requires a listener to quiet down and incline toward the speaker. Sometimes we need binoculars, microscopes, View-Masters, stereopticons to assist our looking, but mediated or not, miniatures suggest there is more there than meets the eye easily. They suggest there is much to miss if we don't look hard at spaces, crevices, crannies.

Miniatures are intimate. Chopin's *Preludes* were written to be played in parlors, those small, bounded rooms built for private talk, small gatherings, or other miniaturized forms of entertainment like *tableaux vivants,* charades, and flirting.

Time, in miniature form, like a gas compressed, gets hotter. I'll paraphrase here an experiment conducted at the School of Architecture at The University of Tennessee and explored in depth by Stewart in *On Longing*: In this experiment, researchers had subjects play with scale-model rooms 1/6th, 1/12th, and 1/24th the size of full-size scale models. The subjects were asked to imagine themselves at that scale, roaming around the model rooms. Then they were asked to tell researchers when they felt they had been involved with each model for 30 minutes. Researchers found that scale radically altered perception of time, and in direct proportion to scale. For example: 30 minutes was experienced in 5 minutes at 1/12th scale but in 2.5 minutes at 1/24th scale. Stewart calls the compressed time experienced by the subject "private time." *Miniature* time transcends the experience of *everyday time and space* by offering a special way to encounter and measure duration.

The miniature, a working, functioning complete world unto itself, is not merely a "small" or "brief" thing, or a "shortened" form of something larger. Miniatures transcend their size, like small-but-vicious dogs, dense chunks of fudge, espresso, a drop of mercury, parasites. Miniatures do nothing less than alter our sense of, and relation to time and space. Finally, and most strangely to me, miniatures are radically self-sufficient. The beings who inhabit fairylands, those elves and sprites, pixies and trolls, don't usually strive to be our pals. They're distant and go about their business. They don't need us. Their smallness is our problem, or intrigue, or desire. They don't need us, and thus we are drawn to them— as any smitten lover might be, to a beloved who remains so close and yet just out of reach.

$\sim$

A FLASH NONFICTION EXERCISE

The old-fashioned letter provided a space for communion between friends. Upon receiving a letter, one would repair to a place of solitude to read it, to allow the essence of the distant friend to fill up the space. A letter cordoned off a sanctioned area of mind, too, and allowed the lucky recipient to spend a bit of deep time conjuring up the feel of being with a friend. Letters, of course, are miniature forms of being, a whole sense of a person compressed.

I have found it clarifying to read my essays-in-progress in environments that are wholly different than the environment in which they were initially drafted. In this way, I reconstitute the sense of essay-as-letter, even if it's addressed only to myself and is in its infancy. Take an essay you've been working on and read it aloud to yourself in a fresh place. Reading in the car at a red light allows for an urgency of hearing, and a close, fast, focused, intensified listening. Reading in a coffee shop (best if it's in another country) allows for a form of intimacy created by ambient, atmospheric bustling—that sense of being happily on the sidelines. Reading a work-in-progress in a library, a space of enforced silence, can make the encounter feel different, too: almost chatty, in a private, slightly secretive kind of way.

How else do we read letters—and in what ways might those forms of reading inform revision? Well, we carry letters with us and pull them out during the day, at certain moments, when only *that voice* will do, or when we need reminding of a truth, or a story, or news amid the static, or to see again just exactly how X was stated. And then there are the ritualistic gestures of letter-reading: the unsealing, the unfolding and smoothing out, the squinting (if you're lucky enough to be reading a hand-written thing), the pausing, musing, smiling, the refolding and tucking back in—all of which add to the physicality of reading.

Taking an essay along, thinking of it as a letter, with all the attendant epistolary gestures, serves to broaden your receptive repertoire. It's the act of decentering the actual space in which revision occurs that allows for a new intimacy with the work, one that might encourage new insights and *active* forms of response.

This revision exercise is really very simple: take your essay to a completely new and unfamiliar space, read it aloud to yourself, and note what strikes you. Work with a pencil and allow new thoughts in, without censoring them—much the way you might allow new perspectives, new personalities, new dreams and wishes and promises-to-self to emerge when traveling. Very often when we receive a great letter, the first response we have is the urge to write back. I'm suggesting that we can create this sensation for ourselves by engaging with our work in unfamiliar territory, "sending" it to ourselves anew, and creating an atmosphere ripe for a fresh encounter.

A FLASH NONFICTION ESSAY

Augury

That hanging bird in the maple tree: someone might come and cut

it down. Or it might stay and dissolve to bone, blowing through
seasons, snared in a mess of fishing line. It must have happened
just days ago, the bright body's still heavy and pulls the line tight.
If taken down, the absence would mean another's discomfort. And
the space where it swings, once open again, a measure of someone's
breaking point—*a thing too awful to see.* Which is very close to what
I feel, rounding the bend down by the lake, finding the goldfinch
invisibly strung. Caught plunging *up,* as goldfinches will, bobbing
and looping in jittery arcs when alive. How a very wrong thing in-
verts the world's laws, stills flight and proposes air can hold weight.
How weirdly suggestive is hanging and swaying: *this should be fruit,*
the form's ends are tapered, the center's a swell of vesicles, ripening.
Wind should make of it *windfall* soon. But the coming upon, the
space called *come-upon,* with its soft breeze and footpath, torches
the idea of harvest, of gleaning. Detonates "just taking a walk." A
bird pinned in air is a measure of wrongness. Walking can't counter
it. Redirecting attention towards kids won't erase it. Even if moving
quickly past—no progress instills; the sight can't be siphoned from
the scene. The bird's presence impinges, like bait.

But yellow gets to be glorious, too. And its brightness not wholly
awful. Such a yellow scours sight, fattens it. It is uncorruptedly
lemon-like. And the sharp bolt of black on the wing shines like a
whip of licorice. At the end of the path and around the bend, here's
the coming-upon again. The moment itself doesn't close down. Its
brightness is not a slamming door. Yellow's not trying to *make up for*
the end.

Time crests there.

The weather patterns. Fish in the lake. Dogs by the shore with
laughing kids.

Why must a last moment be made so visible? And held aloft! Why
must it dangle, and shift so softly, and keep on making a finality?
From it, light rises. On it light settles. Slippery as tallow. Shushing in
breeze.

I think it's good to stand beneath a thing that means to take
words away. It's good to be in a place where thought can't form the

usual way, and a familiar scene—a bird-in-a-tree—gets overturned. Dissembled. Made into a precarity. Looked at one way: cornucopic. Tilted another, it goes sepulchral. How close those can be.

Someone might come and cut the bird down. Or I will, tomorrow.

And after the bird's gone, what would be there, as I come through the trees and around the bend—what, besides shots of memory? An arch of branches over the lake? A green frame around a spot of blue sky, rowboats in a fringe of rushes, the cattails and milkweed about to burst—and past the tangle, just the lake again?

Once, that spot worked like a bower. I liked to walk there and pause at the turn, and enter it, and feel contained. Then, into the bower rained a bird. Dropped a bird. Now swings a bird. Hangs a bird. Yellow shines and yellow ripens. Somewhere are sparrows in a field, seen and *watched over* the story goes, and counted, even as they fall. But come stand in this clearing, late afternoon, the still lake fuzzed with gnats in the shade, the oak's heavy green branch overhead, and lean just so. Center the goldfinch in the frame, squint a little, hold in sight—a planet, flecklet, blot on sun.

A ripe pear, a portent, an airless balloon.

A being whose falling was noted, was seen, whose end was tallied (by the hand of, if you believe).

An occasion for wondering what it feels like to believe.

—Lia Purpura, from *The Iowa Review*

Barrie Jean Borich

WRITING INTO THE FLASH
On Finding Short Nonfiction's Decisive Moment

I am thinking of a staircase, a bicycle, a resonant suspension of breath.

Chances are you've seen the iconic black-and-white photograph I have in mind, "The Var department. Hyères. 1932," a work of twentieth-century French photographer Henri Cartier-Bresson.[1] The slope of an iron railing. A mottle of pavement stone. The gradual curve of a curb. The blurry wheels and back of a boy on a bike. A flash of motion, by which I mean not the pop of flash photography but rather the photographic image's internal burst, abstracted by gray scale, leaving us with the lingering impression of a moment. "For the world is movement," Cartier-Bresson wrote in *The Mind's Eye: Writings on Photography and Photographers*, "and you cannot be stationary in your attitude toward something that is moving."

When I consider the term flash nonfiction, I think of the nonfiction writer's job of rendering the movement of the world, yet the word "flash"—the part of the definition meaning a sudden, bright, glint of understanding—does not lead me into familiar protracted forms of literary narrative. Rather I turn first to a visual understanding of artistic composition akin to a certain kind of photography, such as that documentary attempt to convey the impression of actuality that Cartier-Bresson, working in a nonliterary discipline decades before the more calculated manipulations of the digital age, called the photograph's "Decisive Moment."

Barrie Jean Borich is the author of *Body Geographic* (2013), published in the American Lives Series of the University of Nebraska Press. Her previous book, *My Lesbian Husband* (2000), won the American Library Association Stonewall Book Award, and she was the first nonfiction editor of *Water~Stone Review*. She teaches at Chicago's DePaul University, in the MA in Writing and Publishing program.

We use the term "flash" to describe short short prose forms not only because our experience as readers of this work passes in a flash, but also because of the flashiness of the form's nature. The flicker, surge, and lyric flush of flash nonfiction comes not from the plot of action across time, nor from the exhaustion of observational, intellectual, exploration. Nor is the short short made entirely of linear narrative's opposite: the spare space, breath, and architecture of minimalist poetics. Flash nonfiction, or short shorts, or short lyric impressions may contain all of the above, but the best come to the reader in their entirety, needing no context nor familiarity with formal tradition, more like a photograph of the Cartier-Bresson sort, in which a telling experience or happening is not just expressed but masterfully and intuitively framed.

Most short shorts are not written in a flash. If we are essayists, our first instinct may be to keep adding more, making more connections, applying yet another angle on a metaphor. If we are literary nonfiction writers who've come to prose from poetry we may have taken up creative nonfiction in order to inhabit more space on the page than is usually possible with a poem. As storytellers we may wish to bring forward backstory, wander into history and context, proceed into what happens next, next, and next. Flash nonfiction allows us no such luxuries. Consider again that a short short's flash of literary actuality may expand, occupy our visual field, fill a whole horizon, a whole page even, in a snap, but we won't really comprehend until the movement moves on, a shadow burned into memory.

Human understanding is often burst-like. Lives flash, mesmerizing in the moment of ignition, the same movement that later takes much longer to remember and interpret than it took to live. The Decisive Moment in literature is not just the rendering of some small space of time, but also some slant verbalization of all that the moment conveys. Cartier-Bresson's bicycle evokes so much within the limits of the photographic frame—human hurry, the passage of time through a day, the tension between observation and action, the wheels and cut stones and other

---

[1] Cartier-Bresson, Henri. "FRANCE. The Var department. Hyères. 1932." Magnum Photos. Web. 28 March 2012. http://www.magnumphotos.com.

simple technologies of cities, the accidental beauty of human making. Cartier-Bresson was both constrained and gifted by his tools and traditions—the street photographer's discipline of finding the image in the camera lens rather than later in the darkroom.

The question then becomes: How do writers accomplish that flash on the page?

The writing of a short short begins no differently than any other writing project, yet the required combination of intuition, discipline, and willingness to work within the limited space of a small frame may be as physical as it is mental. The piece may begin with an image, or idea, or question, or wish—anything to get words on the page; first words that are, more often than not, the wrong words. But from the morass comes the promise, some internal flush that tells us yes, we approach the decisive point of focus.

Perhaps we knew we were writing a flash piece when we began, or perhaps it is this pending discovery that tells us so. More textual compression will come later, in the editing, but the primary tightening happens now, in the full-bodied moment of concentrated composition. We know at this juncture not to progress into story or interpretation or further rumination. Nor do we wish to compress all the way back into poetry. Instead we break to white space, or a list, or an object, or some other surprise we don't want to be able to preordain, because this is where the writer's voice comes in, figuring out not just when but what to do.

In my essay "Dogged," in which I write into my memory of a dog I saw once running toward the Calumet Expressway on the south side of Chicago, I knew I had arrived at the flash of the nonfiction when I was able to break from narrative into image. This was the moment I found myself lingering in a description that came from outside of the moment I thought I was writing, a contrasting image of a dog running for joy, an idea that did not come to me fully until a late draft. I knew from the beginning of my work with this hazy-yet-haunting memory that I wanted to write something akin to a photograph, but every draft was bogged down by industrial or political or familial history, not to mention the sadness I had long assigned to that long-gone dog. In long works we often don't know nearly enough about our subject but in shorts we often know too much. I had to step back far enough from my first attempts to come upon not a continuation but an association, not a decision but an intuition.

When I fell upon a description conveying the opposite of what I thought I was describing, I was surprised to find I was writing about *not* my compassion for a particular creature I may not even remember accurately, but rather the meaning I made of this memory 25 years later, and this opposition led me to the essay's subtext, lifted me from the narrative geography of my material, carried me into *my* Decisive Moment. Such compositional decisions, the "aha!" of finding deep subject, are part choice and part implosion, no words invited but those that are needed. Part dream, part craft, part word count, part embodied immersion. Too much forward motion and I would have written into a full-blown essay. The trick is in the timing.

Describing his notion of the Decisive Moment, Cartier-Bresson wrote, "It is the simultaneous recognition, in a fraction of a second, of the significance of an event as well as the precise organization of forms, which gives that event its proper expression."

The flash nonfiction writer's version of the Decisive Moment comes of noticing, and accepting a subject small and precise enough to be contained in such a brief container. We write into this flash of new understanding, then we gather up and get out before the flash fades.

A FLASH NONFICTION EXERCISE

Return to an unfinished draft or fragment of a short you've been unable or unwilling to finish. Try to determine your central image or question or mood, even if imprecise. Free write, focusing on some concrete image or action, something the opposite of what you have already written. Then, in one sitting, compose the essay again, from scratch. Keep in mind that 750 to 1000-word perimeter (as an upper limit, or a cap you will have to edit back down to) as in this new draft you attempt to incorporate both extremes.

A FLASH NONFICTION ESSAY
Dogged

The dog on the Calumet Expressway was no discernible breed, a good runner the size of a Doberman or Greyhound, sleek and short-haired, dark with russet markings. No collar. The dog ran toward my car as I wound down the ramp toward the old East Side, where I was headed to pick up Little Grandma. The dog sped toward the rumble of rusted sedans and semi trucks, into the far south side speedway. Naked was the word that kept coming to mind. Where was that dog headed, so naked, her flanks heaving?

This was near to twenty-five years ago, and I had already moved away from Chicago to Minneapolis. I must have been home for a short visit—an anniversary or wedding. Little Grandma lived alone in the old neighborhood and didn't drive, her children spread out into the suburbs. We were the closest, her oldest daughter's family, just below the city limits where the knock-off bungalows faded into ranch houses. We were usually the ones in charge of transporting Little Grandma and when I was home I usually volunteered.

It was a yellowish drive, especially back then, well before the housing project towers were torn down and old rail yards made into condo communities, before the Superfund dumps were reclaimed as Harborside International Golf Center and the Calumet was re-named the Bishop Ford Expressway after the clergyman who spoke at Emmett Till's funeral. This was the mid-1980s, when the Daley machine had begun to either re-populate or replicate, but before today's green city cleanup had begun. The air itself on either side of the freeway seemed bruised, the horizon punctuated by the glowering from the remaining steel mill and paint factory stacks, a panorama that taught me, when I was a girl, to understand the world as a bleary, glowing finger painting. And too, it was raining, a dingy squall, the day I saw the dog.

I am, without doubt, a dog person. The dogs I live with today receive wrapped presents on Christmas, sleep in my bed, have been known, on special occasions, to wear hats. Years back, before my spouse Linnea and I adopted our first dog, we rescued strays we found on the street in Minneapolis, putting up signs until their people came to claim them. Once two Golden Retriever puppies showed up at our back porch door on Easter morning, and it was easy for me, a former Catholic, to imagine they were a resurrection gift. We brought them into our apartment and imagined them ours, until some rough-looking young men, either neighborhood gangsters or pretending to be, showed up at our door. This was the year we saw neighbor boys with guns stuffed into their pants, the city papers starting calling the street two blocks over Crack Avenue. The boys leaned up into our faces, letting us know they could see we were lesbians, then accused us of stealing their dogs. We handed the puppies over. A few weeks later we adopted a dog of our own.

I wanted to save the expressway dog too, but what could I do? She was running so fast, headlong into traffic. Even if I could have caught up, who's to know how long a wired-eyed mutt has lived wild, and if she did once hang out with humans, who knows how they treated her? People have all sorts of ways of making dogs mean, and chances are a dog without a collar streaking up a freeway ramp was not running from a house where she got to wear hats. And did I imagine I could put Little Grandma and a feral dog in the same car, and let them wrestle for the front seat? I watched the dog veer toward me; the best I could do was swerve out of her way.

Dogs run. Running seems to be one of the ways dogs know they are alive. My own dogs smile when they run. Dogs running, when they run for joy, are bodies leaping into time, elongating, connecting to grace. Sometimes they even bark, as if singing into the moment. But the stray running toward the expressway was not smiling. Her eyes careened as if to ask *where is god, where is god, where is god?*

What I remember of this running dog is not just the blur of her passage but also the backdrop she ran against, the prairie burned away by heavy industry, the poisons that likely made the cancer forming in Little Grandma's gut, the same landscape that may have led all the girls of my place and generation to develop a smoked-in sense of ourselves. I assign my memory of this dog a female gender not because I could actually make out the details, but because I identify with her pumping muscles, a body in trouble, hurtling toward no good end. Wherever this dog came from, and whatever actually happened on the freeway, each pull of the dog's legs, each scrape of toenails against the grainy asphalt, read to me then, and still reads to me now, as the breathless female strain to keep on living.

This exit ramp circled over and into the avenues that led to Little Grandma's brownstone, a two-flat just a block from the Irondale housing projects where my mother's father started his drinking and my mother lived unhappily until she married my father. A few miles north human technology and ambition extrapolates into the Chicago skyline, but down here, in the place that made the steel that make the skyscrapers possible, human passage is marked by the evidence of detritus, a valley of rust, sulfur stink, and accidental scriptures of scrap. Here, before the coming resurrection that will turn at least some of this wasteland back to green, ran the body of a dog who now, many years beyond her natural life, runs in my memory as evidence, yes, of doggedness, a stuttering light, still alive, still running.

—Barrie Jean Borich, from *Sweet*

Carol Guess

ON CARNIVAL LIGHTS, COMPRESSION, AND MICE

My father loved mice, but he also loved me. What I understood of his vocation was a room like my childhood bedroom, filled floor to ceiling with books and baby animals in cages. I don't remember how I came to understand that the mice my father studied were injected with disease. But on the occasion of a dinner party for his colleagues, my pet mice disappeared.

"It's a secret," I told my mother, refusing to divulge their whereabouts. "Don't tell Daddy's friends or they might steal my mice and make them sick."

Childhood was a world of fine lines, careful distinctions. My father and I had mice, but they weren't the same mice. My father even had his own cartoon characters, but their seriousness was never in doubt. There was a t-shirt emblazoned with a giant chicken, the words "POX BUSTERS" printed below. It looked like the t-shirts I wore in grade school, but represented his work on the chickenpox vaccine. As I grew older, I stole his sweaters and tattered corduroys. I stole his gestures, so in photographs we are sitting at the same angle, our arms and legs crossed the exact same way. As a girl, I wanted to emulate my mother—the model, the gifted hostess—but that veneer always wore off, revealing the awkward introvert beneath.

My father the scientist had an uncanny ability to move toward a fixed point—the beautiful solution—with blinders on. He moved with speed—ambitious in the best sense, meaning ethical—driven by both curiosity and empathy. He moved undeterred by distractions around him. And if

Carol Guess is the author of ten books of poetry and prose, including *Tinderbox Lawn* (2008) and *Doll Studies: Forensics* (2012). She is a professor of English at Western Washington University, where she teaches queer studies and creative writing.

by distractions I mean me, I also mean corruption and cruelty, pettiness and bureaucracy. He had integrity, my father, and street geek style. He arrived at meetings in mismatched socks, threadbare sneakers, and corduroys he'd purchased in high school. He often ate family dinners standing up. He had eaten standing up in the Navy and the habit stuck, plus it allowed him to read.

My father the mathematician moved unswervingly toward the elegant answer, toward numbers so bright in the distance that he forgot to look both ways for cars.

"You must," said my mother once, "look both ways for him when he crosses the street."

And so I became Janus, their New Year's baby, a good girl with one bad girl foot off the curb.

My father's work in science and math is often described by his peers as elegant. Often that's the one aspect of his work that I can understand. It wasn't for lack of trying that I did poorly in math and science. No matter how many hours he spent helping me with my homework, I couldn't separate numbers from the fingers I used to count, or stop terminology from sliding, words losing meaning as they rolled toward music.

After years spent trying to choose between conflicting interests, between the elegant abstractions of math and the inelegant but ethically-motivated drive to heal humankind, my father reconciled them in epidemiology, which allowed him to live in the beautiful, poised world of numbers while striving, still, to heal the sick. To cure the flesh without touching the flesh—to tell the story without telling a story—to express emotion without actually feeling—my father wanted the essence of the thing without the dirt. He wanted the view from a window, a smooth pane of glass between the world and his gaze.

My father was prolific in each of the fields he entered, writing articles that engaged with, and often generated, the questions of his day. But he did not write books. Books are rare in his field, a field where speed and wide distribution are necessary for advancement.

"Medicine," he said, "doesn't wait for the book."

Because he and his peers did not write books, they had a fascination with, and maybe envy of, writers who produced them. My father spoke with bewilderment and awe of a colleague who had published several books. When I pointed out that his books weren't serious—weren't groundbreaking and intellectually challenging like my father's articles—my father shrugged.

"But Cal, they're books. You can hold them, set them on the table. You can wrap them in paper and give them as gifts."

When at last my father co-edited a book, he and I both found it funny that the subject of the book was placebos. For years my father and I had engaged in a running joke about medical conference souvenirs, each of us trying to outdo the other by thinking up garish, inappropriate themes for tote bags and mugs. The joke began when my father arrived home from a conference on prostate cancer bearing an enormous coffee mug embossed with a multi-colored image of an oversized prostate.

My mother was horrified, and begged him to get rid of it. I saved it from the garbage that day, and from then on my father delighted in bringing me the most ridiculous freebies he could find. My favorite was a gold pen with "VIAGRA" printed in bold letters, which I use in faculty meetings when I'm having a tough day.

"You're lucky I didn't get you a luggage tag," he told me. "The stats on stealing luggage with Viagra tags are pretty high."

When *The Science of the Placebo* was published, my father joked about what sorts of freebies might accompany its distribution.

"How about a coffee mug without a bottom?"

"How about pens with invisible ink?"

My father was proud of his book, although he never said so. Pride was high on his list of sins. I could tell only because he gave me not one but two copies of *The Science of the Placebo*. The book is hot pink, and I'll admit the cover is not the most attractive thing about it. It has two profiles juxtaposed on the front, presumably to suggest the notion of ghosting that placebos embody. Inside, the articles tend to the topic of medical ethics with seriousness, but also grace. I sense my father's presence as an editor simply because I can actually read the articles and make sense of them.

My father hated jargon. He loved simplicity in language: clarity, compression. He co-edited this volume with a Kleinman, a Kusek, and an Engel, and I wonder if they shared not only his integrity about the ethics of scientific inquiry, but his obsession with clarity and compression as well. Sometimes when I miss my father I am tempted to try to talk to Kleinman, Kusek, and/or Engel, to ask them for anecdotes, odd little bits about his character. Instead I open the book at random and find words I like: "deceptive administration," "voodoo death," "equipoise." My father would have liked these words, too, and we'd have punned around with them, creating new meanings.

I inherited both my father's introverted nature and his obsession with the aesthetics of compression. They seem related, concerned with shutting things out. It gives me great pleasure to pare sentences down, to make stories smaller, more private, contained. I feel so much—too much most days. I prefer being alone to almost anyone's company. The world is a great carnival of flashing lights, whip cracks, and popcorn smells that trail me home, stuck to the hem of my skirt.

When I write, and especially when I revise to make things tiny and perfect, I make amends for my introversion and awkwardness. I am forgiven my unwillingness to socialize. When I write, I take the overwhelming world and winnow it into a window, from which I can see you, but you can't see me.

Of course, there is no craft without content. There is no relation to compression without a relation to release. Compression is the opposite of excess, which means that an emphasis on compression's precision, perfectionism, and delicacy is haunted by traces of its reckless, garrulous, sexy sibling.

Compression, meet Passion.

But that is an essay for another time.

◦⁓◦

A FLASH NONFICTION PROMPT

For now, short and to the point: pare it down to yield new meanings. Not only the sentence itself, but the subject. Here I condense my father's life, and my complex relation to him, to the required word count of below 2,000 words. Compression is the art not only of crafting minimalist lines, but also of capturing a long story by honing in on a moment or detail.

Your assignment is to capture someone who raised you, whether overtly or in stealth, whether well or badly: parent, guardian, swim coach, minister, math teacher, bad girls on the stoop. Capture them by describing a telling moment or detail. Compress a life's worth of memories; allude to the gifts they gave or the damage they did. Give the reader a flash, a glimpse, a photograph. By compressing your story, which self do you reveal?

A FLASH NONFICTION ESSAY
Little Things

My mother's dollhouse has become a constant reminder of something—what?—in the time we spend with her, if it could be said to be spent. At 89 she remembers very little. She does not so much talk as chime, like a clock with a surreal burden: Do we have anything to eat for dinner? Yes, chicken. Do we have anything to eat for dinner? Yes, chicken. For dinner? Yes yes, chicken. Do we have anything. Yes. There's something we have.

This however explains nothing about the dollhouse, which I bought her 30-odd years ago, though she has no idea anymore that that's true. It's a nonce fact from the haze of our family, the kind that only one of us knows, and therefore no one does. She wanted a dollhouse badly though I don't recall how I knew that; she has always been an amazingly taciturn woman. Though my son is 12 and disgusted by all things girly, before we come my mother guards against him by wrapping a bungee-cord all the way round the dollhouse. My mother's decor—Victorian, with teeny candelabra, petit point chairs, a grandfather clock with real brass—reflects a taste as far from her own house as the regal Victoria would be from one of our own lewd and ineptly corrupt politicos, an Ensign or a Sanford. My parents' house in northern New Jersey screams 1970s: flocked wallpaper, shag carpet made of burnt orange, avocado and brown twists—a sea floating the island of gold floral couch.

Is the dollhouse the home she always wanted, I wonder, and if so, why has she chosen so capriciously not to have it? My father wouldn't really care if she switched to delicate petit point and hardwood floors, though he might find it weird. It may be the alchemy of family, where the dollhouse forms a philosopher's stone and we an intransmutable lead. It may be the good home can only be small, small enough for fingers to glue whatever breaks, for survival to be as simple as bungee cord.

Once when my son was a toddler (and my mother had her mind still), he opened the dollhouse doors. My mother caught a glimpse from the kitchen, above the semi-basement room where she keeps her dollhouse. She screamed for him to stop, and rushed so fast and so careless she sprawled down the stairs. At the age of 80, she splayed moaning on the floor in front of the double doors of the dollhouse, looking in, presumably, at waxed wood, at a nickel-sized clock face, its minute and hour still glued where the maker chose.

My father began screaming. At me, my brother, my husband, my son.

He grabbed my mother by the arms and began dragging her, to where. Who knows.

"Don't move her," said my brother. "She could've broken her back."

At which my father dropped my mother and turned on him.

"Don't tell me what to do!"

I recall this in somewhat nonsensical fragments: my brother told my father to stop being a bully, my dad yelled, "I am a bully," waving a fist. I'm not sure how this related to or was intended to help my mother, lying on the floor with her dreams of Victorian respectability, kitchens without food, nursery without children, so close it must have been larger than life. I grabbed my baby and rushed him upstairs, in case things got any worse. My mother, it turned out, had only a few bruises.

It's sad, though my parents love my son, as the saying goes, as

much as they can love him, and who am I anyway to point fingers?
I have my things. My excellent Swiss Army knife that comes with a
teeny flashlight, my cell phone, a few pieces of art I would rather not
have Nerf darts hanging from.

   It's sad in a larger way, dark and liquid, like hooded eyes, or the
sky at a certain hour, or evolution. We know, from chimps and Cale-
donian crows who scoop insects with formed twigs, from the memory and expectation of cats and dogs, the paintings of orangutans,
we share most if not all of what we are. Tool use, thought, beauty. Yet
who whips their young from their doodads and facsimiles? Lies in
the past, face-in? I have seen my mother in the kitchen miming putting on the kettle, absent water. Homey, concrete, here, empty.

                              —Susanne Antonetta, from *Brevity*

Bret Lott

WRITING IN PLACE

For some reason—call it a kind of literary filial imprinting, what duck-lings do when they're hatched and follow only their mother—the books I read when I was in my twenties and in grad school are the ones I hold most dear. My favorite books remain the ones I encountered when I was a student in a strange land called UMass Amherst, where everyone I knew read every book they could get their hands on, and where all we ate, drank, slept, and breathed was writing and writing and writing. Raymond Carver's *What We Talk About When We Talk About Love* was a book I found back then, and one that changed my life. Marilynne Robinson's *Housekeeping* was another, as was Jayne Anne Phillips's *Machine Dreams*. Another was Tobias Wolff's novella *The Barracks Thief*, which I read when it appeared in *Antaeus*, the subscription to which remains one of the most meaningful birthday presents Melanie, my wife of 31 years, has ever given me.

An anthology of stories called *Matters of Life and Death*, edited by Wolff, is one of those books as well. Published by Wampeter Press in 1983, the collection features stories from Carver and Phillips, along with work by Joy Williams, Ann Beattie, Richard Ford, Richard Yates, Stepha-nie Vaughn, Ron Hansen, Barry Hannah, Mary Robison, and John Gard-ner. The book gave me my first doses of what would become some of my

Bret Lott is the author of fourteen books, including the nonfiction works *Fathers, Sons and Brothers* (2000) and *Before We Get Started: A Practical Memoir of the Writer's Life* (2005). *Letters and Life*, his collection of essays on being a writer and on being a Christian, will be out in 2013. He has served as editor and director of *The Southern Review*, has spoken on Flannery O'Connor at The White House, was appointed a Fulbright Senior American Scholar to Bar Ilan University in Tel Aviv, and is a member of the National Council on the Arts. He teaches at the College of Charleston, where he is nonfiction editor of *Crazyhorse*.

favorite authors, and when asked about influences on my writing life, I name this book as a primary one.

So what does all this talk about fiction have to do with flash nonfiction?

This: The title of that collection has stuck with me—has filially imprinted itself on the whole of my writing life.

I believe that every time I put a word down with the intention of making something to last, whether a story or novel or essay, I am inside a moment in which I had better be attempting to wrestle with a matter of life and death. I believe even the sheer *act* of writing is a matter of life and death, that if I am not here in my place and writing, that I am not seeking with the means I have been given—an ability with the written word—to find meaning that will matter.

That book of Wolff's sits on my desk, along with all the other totems I keep in place, to remind me of who I am, of what matters to me, and of why I am trying to write in the first place. Because where I am sitting when I write is the sacred beginning of any attempt to make concrete via words those matters of life and death the worlds inside my own books seek to explore. I keep that book here, because I want to remember why I am here, and why this whole writing thing deserves my deepest attention, and my innermost focus.

Words and what they can do are important.

I believe that seeing writing as a matter of life and death is perhaps at its most acute and necessary when it comes to flash nonfiction. Montaigne's dictum "Each man bears the whole of man's estate" sums up perfectly—how else might it become a dictum?—the purpose of an essay's examination of the self: the reader will, if the author has been honest enough and artistic enough, find within the author's life his own. I have written elsewhere that the form known as creative nonfiction is something akin to Russian nesting dolls, one person inside another inside another. But instead of finding smaller selves inside the self, the opposite occurs: we find nested inside that smallest of selves a larger self, and a larger inside that, until we come to the whole of humanity within our own hearts.

Flash nonfiction is an absolutely compressed form, one in which, using as few words as possible, the whole of man's estate ought to come springing forward, the smallest of nesting dolls created by the author holding inside it the reader's entire life. The smaller the package, I hold, the more acutely that matter of life and death ought to be touched upon, almost as though in the couple hundred words I am giving myself there ought to be an explosion of recognition, a burst of self-awareness that gives my reader the understanding that these few words she's read have had hidden within them a realm far larger than any she could have imagined.

Sounds easy enough. But of course it's not. If it were that easy to pull off, there wouldn't be this subset of nonfiction called flash nonfiction.

I believe, too, that there is no better place from which to touch upon the matter of life and death through flash nonfiction than the familiar sacred places within one's own life, and to write in and of those places.

We all have different places in which the world seems to present itself in its mystery and beauty, its sorrow and grief, its vast breadth and its ultimate intimacy. And because all these places are different—mine will never be yours and yours will never be mine—this sacred place is ripe for exploration, and ripe for sharing. For where else on the planet are you more you—are you more a partaker in the whole of man's estate—than in that place where you are alone, and you are simply and complexly and utterly you?

The propensity we have for regarding such places is that we tend to forget their detail, their texture, their specificity, and the web of associations such places bring us, precisely because we are so familiar with them. I have spent literally thousands of hours at this desk writing books, and most every time I am here I forget I am here, despite the orange highlighter pen that has been lying on the desktop for years now, and the koa wood turtle the size of my fist I brought home from Hawaii in 2000 and that has been on the desktop every day since, and despite the same old tangle of wires that leads from the back of my computer to various destinations both above and beneath the desk itself.

But if what the poet Paul Valéry wrote is true, that "Seeing is forgetting the name of the thing one sees," you can, if you look closely enough at that place where you are seeming to touch upon what is most important to you, discover a new world, first for yourself and then for your reader: you will recognize you, and your reader will recognize him- or herself.

A few minutes ago, right here at this desk, I pulled from the rack of 21 books on my desktop my copy of *Matters of Life and Death*, and thumbed through it.

Here, on page 87, in Barry Hannah's story "Testimony of Pilot," is a passage I highlighted—with a yellow pen—nearly 30 years ago now, back when I read it the first time: "Memory, the whole lying opera of it." This is the first I have taken note of that highlighted phrase in I don't know how long; they are the only words in the whole book I chose to highlight. And now, as I think upon that act of highlighting a few words so very long ago, I am being given again the surprise snapshot of me, a kid in his twenties recognizing perhaps for the first time the grandiose and hollow ways memory can work, and highlighting this realization because he wants to be a writer, and one of the greatest tools, however untrustworthy, a writer can have is his memory.

I am being given once again, through the cloud of three decades of books, and three decades of teaching, and three decades of marriage and parenthood and sitting at my desk, the gift of me.

A FLASH NONFICTION EXERCISE

Sit down in a place you know well and that you hold in its own sacred worth: the back porch, a child's room, your parents' kitchen, the apse of a church, your writing space. You know this spot even as you are reading this sentence. I'm not talking about a lanai on Maui you once spent a lazy afternoon in, but a quotidian place, a regular place, a place you go to all the time, but which still carries its importance within you.

Examine this place, what you see before you, whether it's a desk cluttered with possessions accrued by dint of accident or purpose, or a vista barren save for rocks and sky. Pick three specific elements from what you see, and describe them in detail but without lingering.

Then examine how it is they correspond one to another; try to understand why it is they are the elements you have chosen, what associations they bring to you, and how they serve to illuminate

why this place is important to you, and why being here—here—is a
matter of life or death.

A FLASH NONFICTION ESSAY

On My Desk

I write every morning, getting up at around 5:30 and going upstairs
to my office, where there sits on my desk a vial of red Georgia dirt
I got from the ground beneath the front porch of the farmhouse
where Flannery O'Connor, my hero, lived her last years and where
she wrote most of her work. A piece of land called Andalusia, just
outside Milledgeville. I keep it on my desk to remind me every time
I look at it of something she said about being a writer: "The fact is
that the materials of the fiction writer are the humblest," she wrote
in *Mystery and Manners*. "Fiction is about everything human and
we are made out of dust, and if you scorn getting yourself dusty,
then you shouldn't try to write fiction. It's not a grand enough job for
you."

I also have here on my desk a ceramic tile that serves as a coaster
for the coffee cup I bring up here. There's a picture on the tile,
painted by my older son Zeb when he was six or seven—he's now
26, a Cavalry Scout in the 101st Airborne who has served a 15-month
tour of duty in Iraq—that depicts a lighthouse and sea and sun and
green hills, though you wouldn't know that to look at it. I only know
it because he told me that's what it was when he gave it to me for
Father's Day all those years ago. Next to the lighthouse is the word
"Papa" in orange, though he has never once in his life called me
Papa.

Next to that is a clay coil pencil holder made by my younger son,
Jacob, who is now 23 and living and working in Washington, D.C.,
when he was four or five and spending his days at Little Learner's
Lodge in Mount Pleasant. But the coils that make up the holder
simply aren't piled high enough, so that the pens and pencils tend to
tip over and fall out every time the thing is moved.

Still, I keep my pens and pencils in there. And I put my coffee
cup on that tile inscribed with a nickname I've never gone by, and I

look at that vial of red Georgia dirt, all to remind me every time I sit down to write that time is fleeting, and that I am not here long, and that we are all made of dust, and so I'd better write well, and write what matters.

—Bret Lott

Brenda Miller

FRIENDSHIP, INTUITION, AND TRUST
On the Importance of Detail

Friendship

It's mid-autumn, and I go to a bookstore café in Bellingham, Washington to meet with two women I don't know very well yet. We'd met through a service-learning program at the university, discovered we all want more writing time, more excuses for writing. So Kim, Marion, and I gather in this café—where the service is surly and spotty—at the table next to the poetry bookshelf. This lone bookshelf is hidden away here on the top floor, almost as an afterthought—poetry relegated to the corner where it takes some effort to find it.

We're not sure how to begin. We sip our lattes, gossip about school. My eyes wander toward the poetry bookshelf, and my hand reaches out to grab a book, *Late Wife*, by Claudia Emerson. I've heard about this book, I say. Do you want to read it together?

Assignment

So we do. And we come back together the following week, excited by her "Divorce Epistles," by the way Emerson is able to return to the past, to pain, to loss, through directly addressing the ex-husband. We all have something in our past to address, some complexity that hasn't been easily resolved, perhaps never will be. So we give each other an assignment.

Brenda Miller is the author of three essay collections: *Listening Against the Stone* (2011), *Blessing of the Animals* (2009), and *Season of the Body* (2002). She is also co-author of *Tell It Slant: Creating, Refining and Publishing Creative Nonfiction*, 2nd Edition (2012) and *The Pen and the Bell: Mindful Writing in a Busy World* (2012). Her work has received six Pushcart Prizes and has been published in numerous journals. She is a professor of English at Western Washington University and serves as editor-in-chief of the *Bellingham Review*.

Write an apology, we say, to someone in your past. An "apology epistle." I'm not sure why we come up with apology. It's just the first thing to spring to mind.

Detail

I sit down at home and write the first words, *I'm sorry...* And immediately the image of that piece of wood in the road comes into my mind. It doesn't arrive with a blare and a bang; it just emerges there in my brain, crystal clear, as if it had been waiting all this time for me to blink it into focus. *I'm sorry about that time I ran over a piece of wood in the road.* I haven't been thinking about my ex-boyfriend, a man I knew 30 years ago, a relationship that had been fraught with alcoholism and emotional abuse. *A pound of marijuana in the trunk and a faulty brake light—any minute the cops might have pulled us over, so you were edgy already, and then I ran over that piece of stray lumber without even slowing down. Thunk, thunk, and then the wood spun behind us on the road.* I had been a young woman, very young, still a child. And so, with the image of this small piece of wood, this roadside debris, the entire relationship comes back full force, everything that had transpired between us distilled into the essence of that road trip across the desert. *Your dark face dimmed even darker, and you didn't yell at first, only turned to look out the window, and I made the second mistake:* What's wrong? *That's when you exploded.* You're so careless, you don't even think, what if there had been a nail in that damn thing, *you yelled, your face so twisted now, and ugly.* And I'm always the one that has to clean it up whenever something breaks.

The essay comes out of me in one piece, in about 30 minutes, one image leading to the next. The first words, *I'm sorry...* led me along, and become the mantra for the rest of the piece. *I'm sorry, I said, and I said it again, and we continued on our way through the desert, in the dark of night, with the contraband you had put in our trunk, with the brake light you hadn't fixed blinking on and off, me driving because you were too drunk, or too tired, or too depressed...* I was always apologizing back then, for what I'm not sure. What am I sorry about? Flash images arise, the way that young girl cowered in the trailer, sorry for so many things. I let them come, I don't censor them, because by now the essay has taken on a life of its own. *I would apologize for the eggs being overcooked, and for the price of light bulbs, and for the way the sun blared through our dirty windows and made everything too bright...* And since I know this will be a very short piece, I won't have to inhabit this space very long—in and out, touching the wounded spot and letting it go.

Intuition

I bring the piece, three copies, to our meeting the following week. We're all a little nervous, so we spend most of our time gossiping before turning to the pages in our hands. I read "Swerve" aloud, and as I'm reading I see what I've really written. I didn't know it until I shared it with them; I had just been following that piece of wood. But now I see that while I truly was sorry about running over it, I was really sorry for subjecting my young self to such a harsh and terrifying experience. And behind it all was the fact that I had gotten into the relationship in the first place out of a kind of penance: guilt over something that had happened to me just before I met him. So the entire time was tied up with apology, with truly being sorry for so many things.

I could never have written the essay deliberately, trying to work with all those complex emotions head-on. I simply had to trust in that piece of wood. The second paragraph came out in one long line, because I couldn't risk stopping: I had to keep going to see where we would all end up. *...and even now I'm sorry I didn't swerve, I didn't get out of the way.* I had to let my intuition guide me to that dangerous place, and that last line needed to hold the force of what I'd learned in the 30 years between the event, itself, and the representation of that event. I was sorry I hadn't swerved to avoid a piece of wood, yes, but I was even sorrier I hadn't swerved to avoid the pain that would come to define those years of my life.

Beginnings and Endings

The brief form made this little essay possible. I had been trying to write a memoir of this time, failing miserably because the weight of the emotion was too fraught, too confused, too easy to veer into revenge prose or a sad form of therapy. Because flash nonfiction is so short, I needed to take only a slice of that time, and from this one cross-section—*I'm sorry about that time I ran over a piece of wood in the road*—I could unravel the rest. This form requires the same attention to language as one would give to a poem; each line needs to carry some weight, and to gradually evolve into more meaning as it goes along. The last line—*...and even now I'm sorry I didn't swerve, I didn't get out of the way*—"rhymes" with the first line, echoing the apology, and yet showing a vast transformation in the narrator's perspective. Though it's only 264 words from the first line, we've come a long way in time and a long way in the stance of the narrator—from a girl who is cowed to a woman who can stand up and see more clearly the forces at work in this relationship. *...I didn't get out of the way.* For a short short piece of nonfiction to work, the opening and ending lines must have this kind of relationship, and bring us farther than we ever imagined a few lines could travel.

A FLASH NONFICTION PROMPT

Write an apology, to someone in your past. Focus not purely on the emotion, however, but on an event, and on an image, your own "piece of wood." See where that takes you. When you are finished, look at your opening and ending sentences. Is there a relationship? Can you form one?

A FLASH NONFICTION ESSAY

Swerve

I'm sorry about that time I ran over a piece of wood in the road. A pound of marijuana in the trunk and a faulty brake light—any minute the cops might have pulled us over, so you were edgy already, and then I ran over that piece of stray lumber without even slowing down. *Thunk, thunk,* and then the wood spun behind us on the road. Your dark face dimmed even darker, and you didn't yell at first, only turned to look out the window, and I made the second mistake: *What's wrong?* That's when you exploded. *You're so careless, you don't even think, what if there had been a nail in that damn thing,* you yelled, your face so twisted now, and ugly. *And I'm always the one that has to clean it up whenever something breaks.*

I'm sorry, I said, and I said it again, and we continued on our way through the desert, in the dark of night, with the contraband you had put in our trunk, with the brake light you hadn't fixed blinking on and off, me driving because you were too drunk, or too tired, or too depressed, and we traveled for miles into our future, where eventually I would apologize for the eggs being overcooked, and for the price of light bulbs, and for the way the sun blared through our dirty windows and made everything too bright, and I would apologize when I had the music on and when I had it off, I'd say sorry for being in the bathroom, and sorry for crying, and sorry for laughing, I would apologize, finally, for simply being alive, and even now I'm sorry I didn't swerve, I didn't get out of the way.

—Brenda Miller, from Brevity

Rigoberto González

MEMORY TRIGGERS AND TROPES

While revising my memoir *Butterfly Boy: Memories of a Chicano Mariposa*, I discovered that there were a number of small but significant moments in the manuscript that were important to me but not to the larger story. These passages were little more than anecdotes, but they surfaced like gems when I mined the memories of my childhood because they carried emotional value. Nonetheless they had to be edited out—a painful process but a necessary one.

As I sifted through these extractions I realized that they could read well as stand-alone pieces. They were, after all, bordering on flash nonfiction: self-contained, compressed, sometimes bitter and not always sweet. I also discovered that within each brief narrative an image or object or symbol held the key to the gravity of the story.

It dawned on me that when I initially wrote these narratives, what came first was not the memory but a particular image/object/symbol that triggered that memory. The separation between the trigger and the memory takes only a split second, but it's important to tell them apart because once that key image/object/symbol is identified it can be used as a trope in the narrative. A trope is an anchor that can keep the narration coherent and even help the writer find a way into and out of the narrative.

Rigoberto González is the author of eight books of poetry and prose, and the editor of *Camino del Sol: Fifteen Years of Latina and Latino Writing*. A recipient of Guggenheim and NEA fellowships, winner of the American Book Award and The Poetry Center Book Award, he writes a Latino book column for the *El Paso Times*. He is contributing editor for *Poets and Writers Magazine*, on the Board of Directors of the National Book Critics Circle, and is an associate professor of English at Rutgers—Newark, The State University of New Jersey.

As citizens of the world, we stumble upon images/objects/symbols at every turn and usually by happenstance. But as writers we latch onto the shiny little finds that unlock our memory banks, polish them, and place them at the center of a showcase.

Once I understood the trope as a tool, I went back to the extractions from *Butterfly Boy* and crafted them as if they were meant to exist independently of the longer work. The beauty of these flash nonfiction pieces is that they gesture toward the issues I explored in my memoir—migration, sexuality, education, depression—without coming across as simply samples or excerpts of something bigger. If the artistry is there, so too are depth and completeness.

In this way, flash nonfiction is more like a prose poem whose voice speaks from an autobiographical "I," whose vehicle is sensory imagery, and whose tenor is emotional experience.

Flash nonfiction pieces that function through a single sensory image will give new meaning to that image for a reader. The responsibility for the writer then is to craft a memorable narrative. Those who write poems already have plenty of practice channeling their creative energy onto a single page. And those who work with more expansive terrains will have to readjust the scope and size of their narration.

The labor in writing flash nonfiction will not be taxing if the writer has the three necessary ingredients: a memory charged by an emotional experience, an image/object/symbol that's inextricably bound to that memory, and an editor's chisel to chip away at the excess detail, dialogue, and description.

As I continued to write more flash nonfiction pieces, I began to appreciate the genre's versatility (some were more poem-like, others more prose-like), its brevity, and its proud attention to language. I no longer thought of the genre as merely a second chance for discarded material. The form is a direction for those instances when a writer wants to highlight and celebrate a moment of awareness or awakening that will resonate for a lifetime.

A FLASH NONFICTION PROMPT

Recall a memory that has emotional (not sentimental) value for
you. To differentiate, an emotional response is attached to reason
or thought and makes you ask (and want to answer) who, what,
where, why, and how; a sentimental response is attached to feeling
and simply asks those same questions without seeking to assess or
investigate them. Now think about what image or object or symbol has become the memory trigger of that significant moment of
conflict, crisis, or trauma. As you reconstruct the narrative, allow
that image/object/symbol to become the center of the narrative. Let
the memory trigger become another character in the story and let it
carry the weight of the narrator's emotional journey.

A FLASH NONFICTION ESSAY

Toy Soldier

I am allowed to take only three personal possessions to El Norte. We
will be traveling by bus for three days and two nights, my mother,
my brother and I, to meet with my father and grandparents at the
U.S.-Mexico border. My mother packs our clothes. My brother
makes his selections but he refuses to show me—those three things
are the only things that are only his and he wants to keep it that
way. I choose a green car, a Beetle that looks like a plastic honeydew
melon; *The Little Drummer Boy*, a book with a gold spine; and a toy
soldier, but a giant among the smaller armies of soldiers that my
cousins knock down by rolling marbles across the kitchen floor.

"Why are you taking this thing? It takes up too much room," my
mother says.

The soldier poised with a pointed rifle is a clunky L in my suitcase.

"Because," I say, "I want to impress those Americans. I bet
they've never seen anything like this."

My mother raises her eyebrows but packs the soldier and I'll remember him that way, snug among my shirts and socks, resting his
weapon all the way to another country. I will understand his loneli-
ness when, once we settle in our California house, he gets tossed

inside a box with a book and a miniature car for company—all three objects going cold next to the refrigerator when the lights go out and the night doesn't feel like home.

—Rigoberto González, from
Autobiography of My Hungers

Anne Panning

PAPER CLIPS, SAUSAGE, CANDY CIGARETTES, SILK
"Thingy-ness" in Flash Nonfiction

Recently I attended a poetry reading where the writer mentioned that one of his poems had been inspired by a box of paper clips he'd bought while living in France. His comment got me thinking about all the little things—so often ordinary, everyday objects—that can inspire a writer and send him off running to the computer. As Horace put it, "Much is in the little."

I find the use of objects, or what I like to call "thingy-ness," crucial when writing flash nonfiction. Unlike in short fiction (think Ann Beattie's story "Janus" in which a small white bowl ends up speaking volumes about the protagonist's failing marriage and her affair—though over the course of several pages), brief creative nonfiction utilizes "thingy-ness" in a wholly different way. It relies on *active* imagery—that is, the object must be set into motion by someone or something. It's most successful when the writer avoids static meditation on, say, a grapefruit, and instead sets the grapefruit in motion by having it be tossed across a room by an angry child, for example, or carefully sliced into by a dying grandfather. There simply isn't enough time in flash nonfiction for an object to take on meditative weight without an active force behind it.

In one of my flash essays, "Vietnam: Four Ways," each small para-

Anne Panning's short story collection *Super America* won the 2006 Flannery O'Connor Award for Short Fiction. She has also published another collection, *The Price of Eggs* (1992), as well as short fiction and nonfiction pieces in places such as *Beloit Fiction Journal*, *Bellingham Review*, *Prairie Schooner*, *New Letters*, *South Dakota Review*, and elsewhere. Three of her essays have received notable citations in *The Best American Essays* series. She has just completed a memoir, *Viet*Mom: An American Mother of Two in the Mekong*. She lives in upstate New York with her husband and two children, and teaches creative writing at SUNY-Brockport.

graph presents an object as its focus in an active way. For example, in its first section "Silk," the narrator fingers through bolts of silk at the fabric market, which reminds her of her mother. The following verbs move the object along actively: *shimmers, billows, squints, spins, tucks, measures, pinches*. Similarly, in another of its sections, "Ice Bird," a street vendor makes the narrator's young son a shaved ice bird, despite the tropical heat that melts it. It's the following verbs that set the object in motion: *beckons, cups, blasts, thickens, drizzles, races, rooting, melting*. In both sections, there's an urgency to the narrator's relationship with the object, and a "verby" presentation of such. Surprisingly, flash nonfiction, when written in a "verby" fashion full of "thingy-ness," seems to invite scene-driven writing even in an abbreviated space. In fact, it demands such concentrated active object focus for its punch and power.

Another way flash nonfiction works is by what one of my readers called "sliding"—that is, transitioning between scenes in a way that allows the reader to connect the objects in the essay in an accumulative manner. For example, in Rachel Peckham's flash essay, "The Origin of Sausage," there are eight sections, each leading the reader more deeply into what sausage means to the narrator. Peckham moves the reader through a 4-H project, a butchering at a meat plant, a state fair exhibit, a sandwich the narrator refuses to eat, a pig-topped trophy. The sliding among the various permutations of the object (sausage) is divided by lowercase Roman numerals, but even without them the reader is led in an associative manner that is neither linear nor nonlinear. Instead, it is "thingy" and "verby" in tandem, and, as such, the importance of the object snowballs in a meaningful way. Sliding is important in flash nonfiction, for without it, many pieces could become merely a listing of objects instead of stories that move. The slight white space between sections allows readers to putty in, like a nail hole in a wall, the missing bridge as binder.

Another point about "thingy-ness" in flash nonfiction is that when a writer focuses on a simple object (candy cigarettes, coffee, a white suit), more often than not, that object hands the writer the essay's very structure. This is what I find so appealing about flash nonfiction as opposed to flash fiction: there's something inherently organic about the fusion of content and form in flash nonfiction. There doesn't seem to be a need for an imposed frame when a writer relies on a more natural way of linking or sliding the parts into the whole. For example, my flash essay "Candy Cigarettes" is written in three short paragraphs. The first one begins with childhood, during which the narrator learns to "smoke" candy cigarettes; the next section segues, or slides, into the narrator's adolescence and her mother's attempts to quit smoking; and the third segues to the narrator as an adult who has married a smoker. As I was writing the essay, the specific focus on candy cigarettes led me instinctively to its three-paragraph structure: childhood, adolescence, adulthood.

Relatedly, flash nonfiction often invites an author to use segmentation to further support the sliding technique. When I sit down to write a flash nonfiction piece, very rarely do I ever struggle with its arrangement. If I'm writing about my father's white suit, for example, all paragraphs lead to permutations of that suit: the wedding, the funeral, the mental health institutional whites. Flash nonfiction, despite its brevity, is inherently segmentation friendly. Often what I call the "wheel plot" naturally emerges. Everything in brief essays (the "spokes") points toward and supports the main idea/object (the "axle") and makes the wheel spin. As a result of this singular object focus, I would argue that in flash nonfiction, the opening is not as rigidly fixed as it is in flash fiction, or rather, the opening does not necessarily need to begin *in medias res* the way short fiction does. Instead, a flash nonfiction piece's opening can be informational, suggestive, instructive, or reflective, and the list goes on and on. Instead of asking, "What's going to happen next?" the reader asks of flash nonfiction, "How is it going to happen? And why? And what will it mean to this narrator who we only get to glimpse in 750 words or so?" Essentially, what's important in flash nonfiction is the way the wheel spins, whether it rolls backwards, forwards, back-and-forth, or even diagonally.

Finally, think of the recent spate of single-subject nonfiction books: salt, coal, honey, cod, oil, cotton, the number zero, cinnamon. As I'm listing these commonplace objects, an obvious thought runs through my head: parts standing in for the whole. Is this not metonymy? Actually, the small object standing in for larger idea is more simply put, metaphor—a direct comparison, though blurred around the edges in flash nonfiction.

Ultimately, the point I'm trying to make is that flash nonfiction allows for the small, common object to be used as a means of reaching something much larger—something you might even want to call "mood" or "resonance" or "aboutness," in a way that flash fiction simply cannot.

Recently, my mother died and we've been going through her things. She was a seamstress and a quilter, and I found several Ball jars of buttons I instantly laid claim to. And so my next brief essay, as I scratch it out, will be buttons (the small) standing in for grief (the big). The buttons are my "thingy-ness," which I'll make "verby" to give them life and action, which will then allow sliding as each progression of the object accumulates into something that Poe called "the unified effect."

So open your junk drawer. Dig around in your glove compartment. Dare to be "thingy" and "verby" and brief.

⌁

A FLASH NONFICTION EXERCISE

The ABCs of the Segmented Essay

When writing flash nonfiction, some writers have a hard time grasping how segmentation can derive its energy from juxtaposition. They will often break white space to indicate a slight leap forward in time, but then they often proceed chronologically, which can dilute the true power of segmentation.

One exercise to help alleviate this problem utilizes the alphabet. To start, write the entire alphabet on a sheet of paper, then pick one letter. Make a list of all the things you can think of that start with that letter. (They need not be actual things, but can be ideas, concepts, emotions, etc.) Next choose one of the words from that list and write a brief paragraph about it. For example, you might chose "S," then select "sarcasm" from your "S" list, then go on to write a paragraph about how your father's sarcasm eventually ruined your parents' marriage.

The next step is simply to repeat the previous steps: choose another letter, make a list of words that begin with that letter, select one word from the list, then write a brief paragraph about it. Let's say you choose "T" this time, then selected "trumpet" from your list, then you went on to write a scathing paragraph against high school marching bands. (You may repeat this process as many times as you wish; three times works nicely.) At this point it is helpful to mention Bill Holm's essay collection, *Coming Home Crazy: An Alphabet of China Essays* (Milkweed Editions, 1990), which he structures by using a different letter of the alphabet to begin each chapter.

The next step, of course, is to realize that, although your two to three alphabet paragraphs may not, at first glance, seem to go together, with the right rearrangement and proper juxtaposition, they often can and do work together—quite naturally. So after you've selected "sarcasm" and "trumpet," you might realize that your rant against high school marching bands was every bit as sarcastic as the similar tone your father often used with your mother. Bingo: a segmented essay by juxtaposition is born.

This exercise also works well with other categories: colors, like in Judith Kitchen's book *Distance & Direction* (Coffeehouse Press, 2001), which contains essays titled: "Blue," "Green," "Yellow," "White," "Black," and "Red"; cities, states, or countries; seasons; numbers—pretty much any classification category will work.

Robert L. Root Jr.'s essay, "Collage, Montage, Mosaic, Vignette, Episode, Segment," found in *The Fourth Genre* (Pearson Longman, 2007) is a great resource to further inform this ABC segmentation exercise.

A FLASH NONFICTION ESSAY

The White Suit

My father dreamed of wearing a white suit on his last day of work at Medallion Kitchen Cabinet Factory. "So if you ever see one at a thrift store, Annie," he said, "buy it for me, okay?" I said I would. "Boy, wouldn't everybody look." He smiled at the floor and shook his head. It was his grand vision of greatness, a showy play at humor he'd been preparing for all his life.

My mother went in for a routine surgery shortly thereafter: nothing went right. We watched for a month to see if her brain would flicker back to life. At her funeral, my father wore a dark suit.

Weeks later, my father went crazy. He ran to a neighbor lady's house in the middle of the night. "There are men in white suits sitting on my windowsills!" he screamed. The cops came, the ambulance. I flew home, sat with him in the lockdown psych ward, where he was considered an "elopement risk." They removed the string from his hooded sweatshirt and took his shoelaces. I bought him Dollar Store soccer sandals that kept flapping off his feet.

At night, I held his nervous hands. My father kept asking: "Why are we in a play? How did we become actors in a play?"

He planted a flower in a Styrofoam cup at occupational therapy. His roommate, Dave, was a catatonic who lay flat on his back and told us he'd been committed after attacking his brother with a hammer. It was hard to leave my father there each night.

One day my father got a two-hour pass; I took him to McDonald's for a shake. He wore orange institutional scrubs—the pants high waters, the words MENTAL HEALTH stenciled across his chest.

We sat outside on a metal bench and sucked on straws. The sun shone harsh and hot upon us. "This shake is so delicious," my father said, "it could almost bring a tear to one's eye."

I laughed, almost, and so did he. Almost.

—Anne Panning, from River Teeth

Philip Graham

THE ANT IN THE WATER DROPLET

The memories we have of our lives are not a continuous narrative. Instead, they are more akin to the several arcs of a skipping stone—three, four, five, six splashes and onward. Flash nonfiction is in many ways an ideal form to capture the world of those splashes of memory, fueled by the energy of the previous arc's path descending into the water, as well as, at the end of the brief essay, the energy urging up to the curve of another arc. In this way of thinking, a flash nonfiction piece doesn't have a beginning so much as a point of entry, and a point of departure rather than an ending. In much the same way poetry employs negative space, a flash nonfiction piece can imply and silently give shape to its before and after.

Yet few of us possess photographic memories. If anything, as the days, months, and years pass, we suffer a reversal of those ancient self-developing Polaroid photos: our memories start out clear, and then fade into ghostly wisps. How is it possible to adequately recall the Technicolor details?

Robin Hemley, in discussing Tobias Wolff's seemingly photographic memory in the memoir *This Boy's Life*, writes:

> Wolff reaches back nearly forty years and fishes out whole conversations time and again. The fact is that all writing—whether a letter, a memoir or a novel—requires some artifice. And the act

Philip Graham is the author of seven books of prose poetry, fiction, and nonfiction. His nonfiction includes *The Moon, Come to Earth: Dispatches from Lisbon* (2009), and two co-authored (with Alma Gottlieb) memoirs of Africa, *Parallel Worlds* (1994) and *Braided Worlds* (2012). Graham's nonfiction has appeared in *The New York Times, Washington Post Magazine, McSweeney's, Mid-American Review,* and *The Millions*. A co-founder of the literary/arts journal *Ninth Letter,* he currently serves as the magazine's nonfiction editor.

of writing down memories changes them. They become more real. The line blurs between actual memory and reconstructed written memory so that the writer is less and less able to know for certain what *really* happened. Perhaps Wolff has a photographic memory, or whatever the audio version of that would be, but I doubt it. (*Turning Life into Fiction*, 39)

I doubt it too, but memories don't have to be exact in every detail to contain an emotional truth. The trick is to recapture the details that point to those truths. When my wife, the anthropologist Alma Gottlieb, and I wrote our first memoir of Africa, *Parallel Worlds*, some of the events we recounted were over ten years in the past. In many ways, this was a necessary waiting period. The complexities of living in the culture of West African rural life required a "cooling off period" that enabled us to remember not only specific details, but the significance behind those details. When we recently completed our second volume of the memoir, *Braided Worlds*, we wrote of events that went back twenty years or more. Yet, somehow, many of those memories seemed clearer to us than yesterday's goings and comings because of the emotional intensity of what we chose to write about.

Intensity is even more essential in flash nonfiction, where brevity must be balanced by the gripping necessity to speak.

Memories can also lay dormant, waiting for when you are finally able to remember. One summer residency at the Vermont College of Fine Arts, I sat in the audience while my colleague Sue William Silverman presented her lecture on flash nonfiction. She included a writing exercise, asking us to write about something we'd never written about before. After a few initial scribbles I was nine years old again: 1960, back in the kitchen of my parents' home, on what must have been a Saturday morning, trying to eat my cereal at the circular breakfast table while listening to my mother and father's latest verbal donnybrook.

They argued constantly. The last time I ever spoke with my father, by phone, he was balancing our conversation with a dispute he was conducting with my mother in the background. But of all those arguments, I can't remember a detailed exchange, just the white static of their anger.

Krrrrrsssssssshhhhhhh.

Except for this argument.

I kept my head down as they went at it. But then my father said something that caught my attention. "Y'know, Edie," he said, "I never loved you."

This did not get the reaction I think my father was expecting, or perhaps hoping for. My mother did not break down at his words, but instead replied in a calm, cool tone, "Well, I never loved you either, Bill."

At this, my father left the kitchen. But he returned in seconds, livid, shouting, "Don't you ever, ever say that again!" while my mother faced him unmoved, and began laughing.

Why are these the only actual words I remember of the near infinitude of my parents' arguments? Sue's writing exercise had led me to this unexpected question, and to an answer that further surprised me.

I have no doubt that I heard those exact words (or nearly so), even if I didn't realize their true import beyond the heady fear that my parents' marriage had entered dangerous new territory. Yet that angry exchange must have taught me who loved whom more, and who had the most power because of that. Loving more was a dangerous weakness that could open you up to humiliation. But I also learned that loving less was no less dangerous, that it could turn you cold and vindictive. When it came to love, I didn't want to be like either of my parents. But I had internalized this dilemma without knowing I'd done so, and in my teen years and beyond I brought a hesitance to any possible relationship, a wall of caution I didn't quite understand.

Still, I had remembered the words my parents exchanged; they were waiting for me to listen to them again, saved inside for a reason. As Hemley says, writing down memories makes them more real. Fifty years after that argument a single flash nonfiction exercise offered a greater understanding of what eventually attracted me to the young woman who would later become my wife, a revelation that helped me realize how the carefully calibrated and sometimes contentious balance of our affections has held us together.

How strange—my mind had known the few words I'd need to remember, in order to one day comprehend their long term effect on me. How I wish I'd looked more closely, far sooner. This is what the intensity of writing flash nonfiction can offer: a vivid rather than a casual remembrance. Memories aren't merely simple events easily recalled. The skipping stone of memory lands on a particular place on the lake for a reason, and then ricochets off in a different direction for another reason, and the mystery of those invisible arcs are embedded in the details of the memory left behind. Yet any significance within the details might not reveal itself easily, or it remains there in full light yet isn't ready to be seen. A certain relentless patience, applied to the page, may be all you need.

A FLASH NONFICTION PROMPT

I recently came upon an arresting image, taken by Adam Gormley, an Australian photographer. He had been photographing spider webs when a rainstorm hit, and in the aftermath, he captured an image of an ant trapped within a three-millimeter drop of rain whose surface tension maintained the shape of a sphere. Floating in the middle of that transparent pearl, the reddish-brown body of the ant hunches, its many legs dangling toward the bottom of the raindrop's curve.

Gormley at first thought there was a piece of dirt in the droplet; only when he looked closer did he see the ant. "I shouted out in excitement when I realized what I'd captured by accident!" he said.

Why we remember something is not always immediately obvious. Within certain memories lies something hidden, the equivalent of a floating ant. How to find it? Think of a memory, even a familiar one that you haven't looked at closely in a long time, and examine it as if with first sight, its particular familiar shape transformed by something hidden. Perhaps you will find your memory's floating ant.

While I admire Debra Marquart's flash nonfiction "Hochzeit" because it features accordions and a vivid memory of a polka dance, I especially like the moment when it seems to lift off the floor. The piece begins with a quick image of the author's parents dancing, then moves away, offering a wider view of the long-ago celebration.

Photograph by Adam Gormley, www.adamgormley.com.au.

But then the essay returns to the parents in more detail, and something of the joy of their movement captures beautifully Marquart's evocation of her younger self, seeing them "hold tight, their young, slim bodies enjoying the thrill of almost spinning out while being held in." One brief moment that seems to define a relationship.

A FLASH NONFICTION ESSAY

Hochzeit

I remember circles—the swirling cuff of my father's pant leg, the layered hem of my mother's skirt. A neighbor lady polkas by, the one who yells so loud at her kids every night when she walks to the barn that we can hear her across the still fields. She has a delicious smile on her face tonight, and the creamy half moon of her slip shows under her long, tight dress.

The dance hall is an octagon, eight sides squaring off in subtle shades to a circle. The Ray Schmidt Orchestra is on the bandstand, a family of musicians. The two young daughters wear patent leather shoes, chiffon dresses, and white tights as they patter away at the drums and bass. Their mother, her lips a wild smear of red, stomps and claws chords on the jangled, dusty upright.

The father and the son take turns playing the accordion, the bellowing wheeze of notes, the squeeze, the *oom-paa-paa*. Years later, this son will become minorly famous—wildly famous in this county—when he makes it onto the Lawrence Welk show. He'll be groomed as the new accordion maestro, the heir apparent to Lawrence Welk, a North Dakotan who grew up thirty miles from here. This is polka country. The accordion is our most soulful, ancestral instrument. Someone is getting married, a cousin? Who knows? Everyone is a cousin in this town. I have a new dress with a flared skirt and a matching ribbon; I get to stay up late. This has been going on for hours and promises to go on for more. Old ladies in shawls, looking like everyone's Grandma, sit around the edges of the dance hall, smiling with sad eyes at the children.

A man who looks like everyone's Grandpa makes the rounds with a tray of shot glasses, spinning gold pools of wedding whiskey. The recipe is one cup burnt sugar, one cup Everclear, one cup warm water. The old man bends low with the tray—three sips for everybody, no matter how small. Sweet burning warmth down my throat, sweet, swirling dizziness. This is Hochzeit, the wedding celebration.

Someone lifts me up. An uncle, an older cousin? I have no idea. He dances me around the circle in the air, my short legs dangling beneath me, then returns me to my seat. The old women are there to receive me. They laugh and pat my shoulders, straighten my skirt.

The music speeds up, the accordion pumping chords like a steam engine. My father clasps my mother's hand and pulls her tight. The dance floor flexes and heaves like a trampoline. Women swing by in the arms of their partners. High whoops and yips emit from their ample bosoms. They kick their big, heavy legs and throw back their bouffants. The building sweats, the accordion breathes.

My father secures his arm around my mother's waist. They spin and reel as they polka circles around the room. If left to itself, gravity could take over, centrifugal force could spin them out, away from each other. My mother smiles behind her cat eye glasses, confident of her partner. They hold tight, their young, slim bodies enjoying the thrill of almost spinning out while being held in. My parents. Everyone says they are the best dancers on the floor.

                                        —Debra Marquart, from *Brevity*

Robin Hemley

THE WOUND OF THE PHOTOGRAPH
A Meditation on the Well-Chosen Detail

Several years ago, I wrote an article for *New York Magazine,* and for the first time in my life a professional photographer was assigned to follow my every step through the day. His name is Jeff Mermelstein and he's widely considered one of the finest candid street photographers in the world. Jeff only uses film—no digital photography for him—and he even had an assistant alongside him whose sole job was to load his cameras and rewind and label film. I hit it off with Jeff and a couple of years later we were chatting on the phone about a forthcoming book of his, titled *Twirl/Run.* The book comprised two photographic subjects: men and women running in urban landscapes (many seemed to be late, hurrying somewhere important), and women twirling their hair. The two subjects seemed to have nothing to do with each other, but he felt the photos belonged together and he was looking for a writer who could create an essay that would inform and complement the photos. I asked him if I could give it a shot.

I love such challenges—similar to the challenge of the poet who marries two disparate images or ideas and creates metaphor. It's what lyric essayists do. While I don't consider myself a lyric essayist as such, I love

Robin Hemley is the author of 10 books and winner of a 2008 Guggenheim Fellowship, The Nelson Algren Award for Fiction, the *Story Magazine* Humor Prize, and many other awards. He has been widely anthologized and has published his work in *The New York Times, Orion, The Wall Street Journal, The Chicago Tribune, New York Magazine,* and many literary magazines. His third collection of short stories, *Reply All* (2012), was recently published, as was *A Field Guide to Immersion Writing: Memoir, Journalism, and Travel* (2012). He is a senior editor of *The Iowa Review* as well as the editor of a popular online journal, *Defunct,* and is founder and organizer of NonfictioNow, a biennal conference on nonfiction writing.

the form, as I love poetry, and I've written and published both. So I took a stab at it. The result was a lyric essay titled "Twirl/Run" that appeared in the small press book and also in the online journal *Drunken Boat*.

Here's the opening to give you an idea of how I started to marry twirling and running into one cohesive essay:

> We're all in our own worlds, but few of us more so than runners and hair twirlers. We twirl our hair absently. We run with scarcely a glance at the rest of the world, those passersby strolling, sauntering, meandering. Real runners care about form, but not us— we run only to get somewhere quickly, not for the pleasure of it, or for our health, but because we must. We do not think about those who observe us because we'll pass them soon enough and forget them. "Where's the fire?" we might overhear as we whiz by. For some of us, the fire is at our feet, always nipping our heels. Tomorrow, this mad dash, this very important date, will be replaced by another—in a week, we will have forgotten why we were in such a hurry today. Lateness does not last. It has a shelf life. You can be fifteen minutes late. You can be an hour late. You can even be a day late to the meeting you thought was on Thursday but was really on Wednesday. But at some point, say six weeks out, running seems useless. You are not merely late; you are history.

After that first mention of hair twirling, the activity's not brought up again for a while, and then two characters emerge: a man running to make a date and a woman absently twirling her hair, already moving on with her life. Of course, Jeff's photos accompany the text. It was my intention for the photos and text to speak to one another, but not serve merely as simple illustrations. But does this make such an exercise fiction instead of nonfiction? I don't think so. A large portion of our lives is spent daydreaming, thinking about future scenarios, about possibilities. If we refuse to allow speculation into the essay then we're closing a door on an important aspect of our lives, the philosophical realm.

A series of photos is its own unscripted essay—the essay happens in the ordering of the photos, and using visual means to spark an essay is not only a novel way to write an essay, but also a highly imaginative and delightful exercise. Take a look, for further inspiration, at John Berger and Jean Mohr's book *Another Way of Telling*. This book contains an essay by photographer Mohr that is entirely wordless, a series of photos of an old woman who lives in a mountain village. Without words, what does it mean? Why does it have to mean? What does a concerto mean? When you listen to music, you pick up repetitions, but you don't usually worry about meaning as such.

For me, photography is the perfect accompaniment to the essay, not as illustration but as inspiration. Another example is Lawrence Sutin's *A Postcard Memoir*, in which Sutin uses his vast postcard collection from the 19th and early 20th century as prompts for brief meditations on his life. An essay accompanying a photograph should go beyond the photograph and vice versa. In David Shields' 1996 book *Remote*, he uses a photograph of himself beside Brooke Shields as a wry commentary on how we want to be related to the famous, even through the dubious portal of a common last name. The photo of the smiling Brooke Shields next to David Shields seems full of self-mockery but also mockery of celebrity culture as a whole.

French theorist Roland Barthes in his classic study of photography, *Camera Lucida*, uses two terms, *punctum* and *studium,* to describe our reactions to photographs. The *studium* is what the photo represents in aesthetic and intellectual terms, wholly disconnected from our emotional response. The *punctum* is what Barthes identifies as the *wound* of the photograph. It's both emotional and individual. The *punctum* for you might be different from my sense of the *punctum* in a photograph. It's a small detail that wounds us: a boy's crooked teeth in a photograph of smiling boys, a man shading his eyes from the sun in another picture.

Why not transfer the *studium* and *punctum* from the actual photograph to the words we use to describe it? In fact, this shift is easily done, and by Barthes himself, though he doesn't seem to recognize this. *Camera Lucida* was his last book, written not long after his mother died. The book is an elegy for his mother camouflaged as a book on theory. He describes searching for a photo of his mother shortly after she died, one that would capture her essence. The search was fruitless until he came upon a photo of her and her brother as young children standing on a bridge in a glass conservatory. He calls it the Winter Garden Photograph. When the photo was taken, his mother and uncle's parents were going through a divorce. He describes the photo but refuses to reproduce it in his book. He writes:

> I cannot reproduce the Winter Garden Photograph. It exists only for me. For you, it would be nothing but an indifferent picture, one of the thousand manifestations of the "ordinary"; it cannot in any way constitute the visible object of a science; it cannot establish an objectivity, in the positive sense of the term; at most it would interest your studium: period, clothes, photogeny; but in it, for you, no wound.

He couldn't be more wrong. In fact, his description is so poignant that of all the photos in *Camera Lucida*, it's the one I best remember. What he has created is the *punctum* through words. For me, the *punctum* is the awkward way in which his mother clasps one finger of her younger brother's hand, in the way that children sometimes do.

I suppose this is another way of pointing out that descriptive details matter. That's a *studium* way of saying it, in any event. I suppose we might even say that this is another way of saying that a well-chosen detail can be all that it takes to connect with the reader. But that would blunt the point. It's the correlation between the literary imagination and the photograph that interests me, that inspires me as a writer.

⁓⁊⁊⁓

A FLASH NONFICTION EXERCISE

Think of two photographs, one that exists or used to exist and one that doesn't and never did, but might have. These photos should be dear to you, photographs of *punctum*, not *studium*. They should not be famous photographs of strangers or celebrities, simply because this exercise has to do with your memory or your family's collective memory. So your photos *can* be from your parents or grandparents.

First describe the photo that exists and then describe the photo that might have existed but doesn't. Perhaps it's a photo that you wish had been taken, a photo at a wedding or a family outing. The trick here is to make both photos seem as though they're actually photos.

After you're finished with your two descriptions, read them aloud to someone. The aim is to fool the listener into believing that the false photograph is real and that the real photo is false. Regardless of your success or failure in this, discuss what aspects of your photos conjured up a sense of *punctum* in the listener and which elicited only *studium*.

A FLASH NONFICTION ESSAY

Twirl/Run

We're all in our own worlds, but few of us more so than runners and hair twirlers. We twirl our hair absently. We run with scarcely a glance at the rest of the world, those passersby strolling, sauntering, meandering. Real runners care about form, but not us—we run only to get somewhere quickly, not for the pleasure of it, or for our health, but because we must. We do not think about those who observe us because we'll pass them soon enough and forget them. "Where's the fire?" we might overhear as we whiz by. For some of us, the fire is at our feet, always nipping our heels. Tomorrow, this mad dash, this very important date, will be replaced by another—in a week, we will have forgotten why we were in such a hurry today, because, well, lateness does not last. It has a shelf life. You can be fifteen minutes late. You can be an hour late. You can even be a day late to the meeting you thought was on Thursday but was really on Wednesday. But at some point, say six weeks out, running seems useless. You are not merely late; you are history.

But while lateness lives within its proscribed limits (fifteen minutes, half an hour, an hour), nothing has ever seemed *this* important in *this* moment of lateness. You can't imagine anything ever having been this important. You will be killed, surely, when you arrive. Spears will be hurled at you and you will die in St. Stephen-like agony, a martyr of time. And so this is why, this is exactly why you don't care who looks your way as you huff by. Yes, you're out of shape. Yes, you feel as though you might collapse on the pavement and never rise again in mortal form—but who gives a flying fuck? She is going to kill you, so you might as well die getting there to meet her.

She has forgotten you, schmuck. See her there at the corner, twirling her hair, as absorbed in herself as you are getting there to meet her. She has forgotten your date, in fact, and at this moment crosses the street, touching her own long blond hair as though completing an electrical connection that you are not a part of, that you will never feel. So slow down, stop, wheeze, hands on knees as you gulp air and watch her walk away *so* slowly, but too fast for you now. You don't even have breath enough to call her name, and would she even hear you if you did—what does she think about as she twirls? Texture, and that is all. The texture of her own cells, her own life, and that is impenetrable. The loop she has completed within herself cannot be broken now, not by you.

Once, in a magazine, she read that hair twirling was an unconscious sign that she was turned on, that she wanted to have sex with the guy beside her. Not as bold as a Krispy Kreme sign, but equally insistent: Hot Donuts Now! The idea made her laugh—some guy, some out-of-shape always-running guy wrote that, no doubt. Yeah, buddy, in your dreams. But that kind of hair twirling—the coquettish I-know-I'm-cute kind of twirl—that's not her style. That's not a true hair twirl, because for a hair twirl to be true, to be authentic, it needs to be liminal, half-aware. No one's written that down, of course. There's no Handbook for Hair Twirlers. But she makes the rules here. It's her hair, her twirl. It will mean to her whatever she wants it to mean.

Self-caress—the fingers feel but not the hair. The hair, unfeeling, but so lovely, so doted upon. Some people focus on their children, some on their pets. But we . . . we love our hair. Really, we should hate our hair, remnant of our monkey past, nagging reminder that we are, after all, not so different from all the other animals. We would not want to be covered entirely in it—hair is not like gold. You can have too much hair. And you can have too little. We want enough hair so that it can be said of us, "Her hair is so luxuriant." It

is up to the fingers as well as the eyes to determine if hair is luxuriant or not. But the eyes are in service to the fingers in this case,
because luxuriant hair needs fingers to run through it.

But we must acknowledge the nervous twirlers, too, those
separated only marginally from the chronic hair pullers, nail biters,
and nose pickers. Look at the nails of the nervous twirler next time
you pass her. Bitten to the quick. Maybe she picks her nose, too. Of
course she does—she is trying to erase herself and hold on to herself
at the same time. She doesn't quite believe she's real and seeks
evidence of her corporeality moment by moment. Twirling her hair
helps her concentrate. Her hair is as close to her brain as she can
ever get—on the other side of that impenetrable wall, that's where
she lives, under that luxuriant cover, that animal pelt.

Do other parts of the body speak to one another as publicly yet
intimately as the fingers and the hair? The hair cascades and dances
as you run. But it will not twirl, Medusa-like, on its own. Imagine
the specter of a woman running, her hair twirling as if twisted by
invisible fingers—or perhaps a drowned girl twisting in the current,
the waters twirling her hair. Then and only then are the hands useless. And my hands are never useless—or at least they're in constant
motion. That's how you can tell I'm alive. Watch my hands. The only
time my hands aren't in motion is when the rest of me is, when I'm
running.

—Robin Hemley, from *Twirl/Run* and *Drunken Boat*

Jennifer Sinor

CRAFTING VOICE

Two weeks ago, I lost my voice. When I opened my mouth, nothing came out, no words, no whisper. I had been sick, so I didn't worry my inability to speak would be permanent. Instead, I stuffed a notebook in my coat pocket and set off to meet the morning. For the next four days I played charades with the world, gesturing for my coffee, pointing to the peas I wanted my son to eat, writing long notes on the white board in hopes my students would understand the glory of the novel before us. Each day I grew more depressed, shrank into myself. What had first been a novelty, even a vacation of sorts from parenting and teaching, started to stifle. Without a voice, I was cut off from everything. Conversations happened all around me while I scrawled notes to make points no longer relevant. I couldn't even call the dentist to complain about the bill.

On the second afternoon, my four-year-old son, not yet a reader, burst into tears when he was unable to decipher my gesture for "get dressed."

"Just use your regular voice, Mama," he cried. "Talk regular."

I couldn't even explain to him why that was impossible.

Voice, I tell my students, is one of the most vital yet ephemeral qualities of writing. We can't point to it on the page, pin it down, say that here, right here, in the way this sentence runs or in this choice of words or in this use of detail, we have voice. Rather, we note its absence by the distance we feel from the writer, from the subject, or from the words on the page; we feel cut off.

Jennifer Sinor is the author of *The Extraordinary Work of Ordinary Writing* (2002). Her essays have appeared in *The American Scholar, Fourth Genre, Utne Reader, Brevity,* and elsewhere. Most recently her work was anthologized in *The Norton Reader.* An associate professor of English, she teaches creative writing at Utah State University.

Not unlike the genre itself, voice in creative nonfiction is best defined by what it is not. Voice is not point of view, although the two are related. When we ask about a writer's voice, we aren't asking about the vantage from which a story is narrated—first or second or third person. We might be asking about the intimacy of that point of view, a distinction Dinty W. Moore makes, but voice and point of view aren't interchangeable. Voice is also not tone or the emotional stance of the narrator toward the material: angry, ironic, remote. A chosen tone may help register the voice, but, again, it isn't the same thing. Nor is it style. An essay can have beautiful, lyrical language and syntax and be devoid of voice. Voice isn't about narrative perspective either—Virginia Woolf's "I now/I then" distinction. Because the narrator tells the story from different perspectives—as a child, then as an adult—doesn't mean the voice changes. The voice remains the same; the perspective switches. Finally, the voice of a piece does not align neatly with the voice of the narrator or a character in the essay. Voice doesn't inhabit a pronoun. The speaking "I" in a memoir or essay doesn't provide the voice, or at least not entirely. When we talk about voice in literary nonfiction, we mean the voice of the writer, the one crafting the narrator, the sentences, the deeper subject. And you can't point to a paragraph or a detail or a line of dialogue and say, there, that is the writer's voice. It exists behind the writing, infusing the prose. In writing flash nonfiction, where every element of craft must be lean and taut, the writer's voice is present from word one.

Thankfully, while voice may be seemingly impossible to point to on the page it is not impossible to practice. Like all other aspects of writing, voice is a made thing. You don't "find" your voice; you make it. While the intimacy of a chosen point of view or an author's style or tone is important to voice, the real work of creating strong voice is work that takes place off the page. It requires focusing on two aspects of writing: internalization of subject and vulnerability in approach.

Knowing Your Subject

When we say a piece has a strong voice, what we are really saying is that the writer fully understands her subject. Not cerebrally, but internally, even bodily. It is not enough to research your past—if you are writing memoir—or your subject—if you are writing research-based literary nonfiction. Well-researched pieces are often devoid of voice. Think of a textbook. To fully understand a subject means to let that subject inhabit you, to live with it, sleep with it, fully know it not in terms of fact but in terms of complication. Only when you fully understand a subject—why your parent's divorce hurt so much when you were 12 or the chemical process of radioactive decay—does that confidence translate to voice on the page.

Look at Brian Doyle's "Leap," given as an example essay after the exercise below. When initially approached about writing a piece in response to 9/11, Doyle replied to the magazine editor, "No, there is nothing to write. The only thing to say is nothing. Bow your head in prayer and pray whatever prayers you pray. There is nothing to say." He felt the subject was not his own. At least not initially. But the events of 9/11 would not leave him, and he began to realize that as a writer the only way he could assemble a life post 9/11 was through meeting the event on the page.

In less than 600 words he tackles one of the greatest tragedies in U.S. history. Three thousand people died. Our way of reckoning time and place forever altered by one morning. What can Doyle say in response? He does not live in New York, and was, like most of us, hundreds of miles away. How would he have begun?

With falling bodies, I imagine, with the newspaper accounts of blood-filled air. I imagine those bodies kept him awake, that they stalked his sleep. I imagine he couldn't put the bodies down, that he dragged them to the shower in the morning, to work, and home again, that the bodies piled behind his students when he conferenced with them, that he tucked the bodies into bed at night with his children. One morning, though, he must have realized he wasn't sure where his body ended and theirs began. They inhabited one another. I imagine it was at that point he began the piece. But not with writing, or at least not only with writing. He finds his way into the story not by retelling an event we saw repeated again and again on our televisions, but by going to the library, to the archives, learning what he could of the people who leapt to their deaths. He researches the science of falling bodies, the names of the dead. He reads first-person accounts, perhaps interviews witnesses, maybe stands in the middle of New York and looks up into an empty sky. He puts his body in motion to understand theirs. And the result of that work—physical work, leg work, as well as reflective work—is an essay that draws us in at the first word and never lets us go. His voice is quiet and confident, as well as urgent and pained, but most importantly it's there. The writer is there, even though the first person initially is not. The writer is behind the prose, leading us through his understanding of the disaster. It is because he has so deeply explored his subject—literally in primary and secondary source material, as well as reflectively in the way he has carried the piece with him though the days—that we recognize an author, one with authority over what he writes. We hear him speaking to us, know he embodies each of the 600 words.

Vulnerability

Doyle's actual body, his "I," does not appear until late in the piece, but it is at that moment that he names his stake in this story, brings forth the sleep-shattered "I." In revealing his investment in the subject, his humanity, we see the second element necessary for crafting voice: the writer's vulnerability. At the moment the "I" enters, the prose changes, signifying the shift in responsibility for the story. He moves from a newspaper accounting of the event—simple sentences pierced by facts, quote-filled lines reporting what witnesses saw—and moves into the lyric, a space defined by emotion rather than reason, a space defined by association rather than chronology, where his sentences tumble across one another, falling like so many bodies down the page, only to topple into a heap at the end, leaving his body holding onto their bodies "against horror and loss and death."

The form of his piece, the way he strings his sentences together, his diction, his images all conspire to name his stake in the story: the human capacity for love. And we join with him in his whispered prayer, unable to ever see the events of that day in the same way again. We now hold those bodies in our own because Doyle was first unable to lay them aside. And because we know that a real body, a person whose humanity replicates our own, is writing, is behind these words on the page, we listen. We hear the writer's voice—not some projection, some flimsy prop—but a person who has been changed by his subject, embodies his subject, just the way his voice embodies the prose, calling us from our sleep.

Time and Practice

Voice takes time. You cannot internalize your subject or name your stake in a story quickly. You must live with your subject, learn its movements, its manners. And voice comes forth through revision, each draft coming closer to what you really want to say. The easiest way to understand voice is to watch it evolve over several drafts—either of your own work or another's. And as Doyle's essay so brilliantly captures, when the voice of an essay is vibrant and strong, the words cannot remain unheard.

⌐ポ⌐

A FLASH NONFICTION EXERCISE

Unlike, say, detail or dialogue or scene reconstruction, it is difficult to practice voice through writing exercises. The best way to work on voice is to simply keep writing, keep discovering your subject and your stake in it. That said, Bill Roorbach, provides a useful exercise in his book *Writing Life Stories*. He suggests that you write a letter to someone you haven't seen in a very long time, explaining yourself. It's a letter you don't plan on sending and can be to someone living or dead. Once you have composed the letter, go back to it and cut out all the throat clearing, the salutation, the small talk. See where the heart of the letter is, the issues, the dramatic tension. Read those moments aloud to a classmate. Feel the strength of your voice. He argues that when we write to a particular person our voices are closest to the surface because we know who we are (at least in relation to the person we are writing). We know the stakes. This kind of knowledge over the material translates to a confident and vibrant voice. It can be useful to think about whom you might be writing an essay to, or even a book-length project. If we have a particular person in mind as we write, our voice is often stronger.

A FLASH NONFICTION ESSAY

Leap

A couple leaped from the south tower, hand in hand. They reached for each other and their hands met and they jumped.

Jennifer Brickhouse saw them falling, hand in hand.

Many people jumped. Perhaps hundreds. No one knows. They struck the pavement with such force that there was a pink mist in the air.

The mayor reported the mist.

A kindergarten boy who saw people falling in flames told his teacher that the birds were on fire. She ran with him on her shoulders out of the ashes.

Tiffany Keeling saw fireballs falling that she later realized were people. Jennifer Griffin saw people falling and wept as she told the story. Niko Winstral saw people free-falling backwards with their hands out, like they were parachuting. Joe Duncan on his roof on Duane Street looked up and saw people jumping. Henry Weintraub saw people "leaping as they flew out." John Carson saw six people fall, "falling over themselves, falling, they were somersaulting." Steve Miller saw people jumping from a thousand feet in the air. Kirk Kjeldsen saw people flailing on the way down, people lining up and jumping, "too many people falling." Jane Tedder saw people leaping and the sight haunts her at night. Steve Tamas counted fourteen people jumping and then he stopped counting. Stuart DeHann saw one woman's dress billowing as she fell, and he saw a shirtless man falling end over end, and he too saw the couple leaping hand in hand.

Several pedestrians were killed by people falling from the sky. A fireman was killed by a body falling from the sky.

But he reached for her hand and she reached for his hand and they leaped out the window holding hands.

I try to whisper prayers for the sudden dead and the harrowed families of the dead and the screaming souls of the murderers but I keep coming back to his hand and her hand nestled in each other with such extraordinary ordinary succinct ancient naked stunning perfect simple ferocious love.

Their hands reaching and joining are the most powerful prayer I can imagine, the most eloquent, the most graceful. It is everything that we are capable of against horror and loss and death. It is what makes me believe that we are not craven fools and charlatans to believe in God, to believe that human beings have greatness and holiness within them like seeds that open only under great fires, to believe that some unimaginable essence of who we are persists past the dissolution of what we were, to believe against such evil hourly evidence that love is why we are here.

No one knows who they were: husband and wife, lovers, dear friends, colleagues, strangers thrown together at the window there at the lip of hell. Maybe they didn't even reach for each other consciously, maybe it was instinctive, a reflex, as they both decided at the same time to take two running steps and jump out the shattered window, but they *did* reach for each other, and they held on tight, and leaped, and fell endlessly into the smoking canyon, at two hundred miles an hour, falling so far and so fast that they would have blacked out before they hit the pavement near Liberty Street so hard that there was a pink mist in the air.

Jennifer Brickhouse saw them holding hands, and Stuart De-Hann saw them holding hands, and I hold onto that.

—Brian Doyle, from *The American Scholar*

Lee Martin

COMMUNAL AND PERSONAL VOICES

In 1963, when I was seven, my family moved from a farm in southeastern Illinois to a southern suburb of Chicago. My mother was an elementary school teacher, and she'd taken a position with the Arbor Park School District 145 in Oak Forest. I didn't want to make that move. I wanted to stay on our farm and keep going to the two-room country schoolhouse that was familiar to me, as were my friends and my teacher.

"People in hell wanting ice water, too," my father said when I protested, and that was that.

He was a gruff sort, but on occasion he could turn sweet. *Honey,* he'd call me sometimes when I was upset over something or the other. *Honey,* he'd say. *What's wrong?*

Both of those ways of speaking, the harsh and the tender, were among the voices that made up my childhood. My father was often blustery and crass. My mother was soft-spoken and discreet. *Mercy,* she'd say sometimes in a hushed voice when she didn't know what else to say. *My word,* she'd say. Or, if angered, she'd use the strongest oath she permitted herself—*Well, fiddle!*

The people we moved among—those farmers, oil field roughnecks, refinery workers, shop clerks, shoe factory workers, short-order cooks, teachers, grain elevator workers, truck drivers, mechanics—spoke a similar language: part colorful and direct expression, part homespun solace.

Lee Martin is the author of four novels, including *The Bright Forever*, a finalist for the 2006 Pulitzer Prize in Fiction, and *Break the Skin* (2011). He has also published three memoirs, *Turning Bones* (2003), *From Our House* (2009), and *Such a Life* (2012). His flash nonfiction, including "Dumber Than," has appeared in *Brevity*. He teaches in the MFA program at The Ohio State University.

Their voices formed the chorus of our rural community, and over the years they burrowed inside me, and now, even though I'm long gone from that place, I can't get them out of my head. They're part of who I am—the voices of that place. They make up a persona that's available to me as a writer of creative nonfiction—particularly when I write in the flash forms, which are often voice-driven.

The voices we use in our writing come from sounds and tones we've soaked up from the people and the institutions around us, particularly when we were young. I'll always have the straightforward tone of my father's voice. I'll also have the quiet, more contemplative tone of my mother's. At the same time, I'll have the sounds of the Church of Christ, which allowed no instrumental music in its services and, consequently, highlighted the verbal music of prayer, the voice lifted in song, the ornate language of the King James Bible. I'll have that as well as the gossiping—the b.s.ing voices in Tubby Griffin's barber shop and the hushed, respectful whispers among mourners at Charlie Sivert's funeral home. I'll have the farm market reports and the local news of hospitalizations and deaths delivered in a monotone on WAKO radio each afternoon. They'll be there, though, co-existing with all the voices I acquired during my six years in Oak Forest, which were different voices that got layered in with those from southeastern Illinois. Everything recorded and ready to be played back in my flash nonfiction as I choose.

In Oak Forest, I heard the voices from other ethnic groups—Italian, Mexican, Polish, German, Russian, Dutch. I heard different sounds in the very names of my friends—*Bettenhausen, Pettke, Lipari, Pigniatello, Pagel, Galeas, Albiero, Dykstra, DeVos, Smykowski, Inczauskis, Modrak.* I heard a hipper, jazzier sound when I listened to the dee-jays like Larry Lujack on WLS radio. I heard irreverent voices from those cool-guy dee-jays, a more worldly, more jaded voice from them and also from the adults around me. One evening, during a sing-along at a school program, I heard our principal's husband alter the words of a song, so he could sing *Little Tommy Stinker* instead of *Little Tommy Tinker*. He was having a great time. He thought it was the funniest thing there could possibly be.

Flash nonfiction often requires a lyric impulse, and when we write from that impulse, it pays to consider ancient Greek drama and how its makeup is similar to a strategy we can use in our writing. Those ancient Greek plays featured a chorus comprised of a group of speakers whose function was to comment on the dramatic action. The voices of that chorus often provided a cultural backdrop from which a single actor spoke, often accompanying himself on the lyre. The verse of this actor was more personal—more lyric—and in this way the drama gave a textured sound of the individual speaking from, and being considered by, the community.

When we write flash nonfiction, we might consider the fact that we all are members of communities, whether they are our present ones, our past ones, or, as is more likely, a combination of the two. Perhaps we speak in concert with those groups, and perhaps we speak in resistance to them. In either case, the vocal influence of our communities is strong.

It also serves us well to know the more personal and individual voice that rises above the voices of the groups. Of course, we have more than one of these more personal voices. We speak from various aspects of our personalities, and, when we do, we hear the sounds that are ours, influenced by the communities from which we've come or the ones where we now reside, but also singular and in some way ours alone. I've always thought of those voices as the voices we hear in our heads when we talk to ourselves. Don't we all do this? Surely, I'm not the only one who has that voice, split into a number of registers and tones, that speaks to the self at various times when I'm my only audience. That private voice.

Becoming aware of both the communal and the personal voices not only gives a more textured sound to our flash nonfiction, it also lends a note of urgency, particularly if the juxtaposition of communal and individual creates a tension in the speaker. This tension helps push the piece along as the different tones and personas rub together, providing the conflict of sensibilities crucial to the quick exploration of subject matter. In flash nonfiction, there's often not enough time and space to rely on the reflective voice common to longer pieces—that voice that creates the meaning as the writer considers, questions, speculates. In a shorter piece, much depends on the close attention the writer pays to detail and language. The tension of tones and personas competing for space demands that the writer stay in the moment—the lyric moment where concrete details, the careful arrangement of words, tone, and voice are so crucial to its success. At the same time, this competition deepens the main character, the writer. We see him or her—at least the persona he or she has decided to express—comprised of the group and yet also distinct from it.

Such is the case in my flash nonfiction piece, "Dumber Than," which begins with the voice of the small southeastern Illinois town where I spent my high school years after my family moved back downstate. The people in our small town could be direct with their judgments of a person. A place also known for its tendency to rely on colorful expressions. I start this essay by speaking in the idiom of that place, speaking from the persona of the townspeople as they pass judgment on a slow-witted boy who lived close to me. He was, in the language of the town, "dumber than a box of rocks," "dumber than dirt," "dumber than a post," "dumber than a bagful of hammers." I use various forms of that "dumber than" saying as the chorus from the townspeople. Then I find a place to tell a more personal story about a time when I caught that boy up to no-good and how angry he made me. My actions make me consider my own culpability in the poor end that this boy came to, but, because of the voice of the townspeople, I turn the essay at the end so I demand that they share in my guilt. The final line about everything we thought we knew about the boy has a hollow sound coming from its certainty, and that textured tone—one of irony—is only possible because I speak from both the communal and the personal.

A FLASH NONFICTION PROMPT

Recall a turn of phrase common to one of your communities and use it as a way of beginning a piece of flash nonfiction. Allow yourself to speak from the persona of the group. Then quickly find a place to step forward and speak more personally. As you turn toward the end of the piece, consider how the persona you've established for yourself is fitting into and/or separating itself from the persona of the group. Be aware of the tensions that exist between different aspects of yourself and how the short piece that you write invites you to do a quick exploration of your own character. Consider how speaking from the voice of the community at the very end of the essay may have a very different sound than such speaking had as the piece opened.

A FLASH NONFICTION ESSAY
Dumber Than

A box of rocks. That boy—oh, you know the one. Dropped his cat from that second-story sleeping porch just to see if it was true, what they said about cats always landing on their feet. Bawled when that tabby hit and bounced, lay dead on the cement walk.

Dumber than dirt.

One day in school, the teacher asked him to name the capital of Illinois. "I," he said, and don't think that one didn't get around—how those kids howled until the windows shook, how even the teacher couldn't stop herself from laughing.

Dumber than a post.

E.T.—that's what folks started calling him. This was way before the movie about the cutesy extra-terrestrial. E.T. for "elapsed time." Whatever went in one ear shot out the other like a laser beam, nothing to stop it. He wasn't all there. He was on a fast road to somewhere no one could see. Wherever it was, when he was dropping that cat, or answering that teacher's question, he was zipping ahead. He was already gone.

Once at Halloween, I caught him soaping the windshield of my '73 Plymouth Duster. It was broad daylight, for Pete's sake, and the car was right there along the street where anyone could see him. He didn't care. He was this big, goofy kid with a bar of Lifebuoy. In a few years, he'd shed his baby fat and become a muscle man. I grabbed him by the arm, asked him what the hell he thought he was doing. He couldn't stop laughing—amused, I like to think, by his own stupidity and how pissed off he could make me. He laughed until he was crying and spitting and his nose was running, and that just pissed me off more. I dragged him into the house, clamped onto him while I used my free hand to rustle up a rag and a pail and fill it with water. "You're hurting my arm," he kept saying. "Hurting my arm." But he couldn't stop laughing. He laughed like an idiot even when I dragged him back outside and told him to by-God clean that soap off that windshield. It was the most joyous sound. He laughed like the Judgment had come and any minute he'd lift up to Heaven.

How was I to know, when I grabbed him by his arm, that one day when he was a grown man, he'd take a golf-club—a five iron—and beat his wife until she was dead? I ask you. Seriously now. How could any of us have known that he'd kill women across three states—at least that's what he told the law. Then, when they asked him for the particulars—how many women, where, what had he done with the bodies—he wouldn't talk. Just dummied up. Wouldn't say a goddamn word.

That's when we got all righteous. Don't act like it's not true. Dumber than a bagful of hammers, we said. Now that's one thing we always knew for sure.

—Lee Martin, from Brevity

Sue William Silverman

WRITING THROUGH INNOCENCE AND EXPERIENCE
Voices in Flash Nonfiction

The "I" in creative nonfiction is a literary device used to enhance and explore complicated truths. Just as we are complex people in life, we must be equally complex personas on the page. One way to accomplish this exploration of self is through the use of voice—but not one's everyday voice. In real life, for example, I don't speak or write e-mails using carefully crafted language. When talking to friends, I'm not particularly mindful about word choice. I don't use sensory imagery or think metaphorically. My speech meanders, full of half-developed ideas. In other words, a spoken, informal voice, though it can be breathless or intimate, is rarely as artistically structured as one that's literary.

Using my flash nonfiction piece "Archipelago" as an example, let's say that, at the time of the actual event (years before I wrote the essay), I confided in my sister as to why I didn't want to leave the West Indies. I would probably have said something like: "I hate leaving. I don't want to live where it's cold." This brief explanation, while sincere, provides little insight or depth.

Likewise, a diary "voice" can be intimate, but it doesn't shape life into art, either. Here is a diary entry I could have written the night before leaving the island: "I'm going to miss everything about St. Thomas. I hate even the thought of returning to the States, where it's so gray and cold."

Sue William Silverman's memoir Love Sick: One Woman's Journey through Sexual Addiction (2001) is also a Lifetime Television original movie. Her first memoir, Because I Remember Terror, Father, I Remember You (1999), won the Association of Writers and Writing Programs award series in creative nonfiction, and her craft book Fearless Confessions: A Writer's Guide to Memoir was published in 2009. She teaches in the MFA program at Vermont College of Fine Arts.

These sentences are heartfelt, but abstract, lacking sensory imagery. They don't bring the reader inside the experience.

Neither of these voices, though they are authentically me, would work when writing flash nonfiction.

So who, then, narrates an essay? It's both me and not me. It's an artistically created "me" comprised of two different voices that work in conjunction with each other: the Voice of Innocence and the Voice of Experience, labels loosely borrowed from the poet William Blake. Briefly, the Voice of Innocence describes the event. The Voice of Experience interprets and reflects upon it. Through the use of these voices, a writer maintains a cohesive narrative, while also journeying into the core of self-discovery. In other words, the voices used in creative nonfiction artistically craft what you've lived, in all its dimensions.

Here is a fuller description of these two aspects of the narrator's voice:

The Voice of Innocence relates the facts of the story, the surface subject or action. It's the voice that tells us, "first this happened, then this next thing happened." Additionally, the Voice of Innocence reveals the raw, not-yet-understood emotions associated with the story's action by portraying the person you were (and what you felt) when the sequence of events actually took place.

The Voice of Experience adds a more mature voice or persona that, in effect, explains and deepens the Voice of Innocence with metaphor, irony, and reflection. This voice offers the progression of thought in creative nonfiction by examining what the Voice of Innocence (facts and raw emotions) means. This more complex viewpoint interprets and reflects upon the surface subject. Say, for example, the Voice of Innocence describes feeling lonely; then, the Voice of Experience seeks to understand why you're lonely, what it means. What are the ramifications of past occurrences and behaviors? What are the metaphors that deepen the events? With this voice you transform the lived moment, rather than merely recollect it.

Generally speaking, these two voices are flexible and can be introduced at any time during your essay, as needed. Now let's see how they actually work within a piece of flash nonfiction.

In "Archipelago," I begin with the Voice of Innocence in the first paragraph, where I state in a straightforward manner that I'm boarding a plane to leave the West Indies. In the second paragraph, I use the Voice of Experience when I reflect upon how, living in the States, I anticipate feeling "static," as if "suspended in ice," waiting to "melt into spring." Because this voice allows me, the author, to go beyond mere facts, I'm able to construct the idea of cold and ice into a metaphor, thus enabling the reader to understand that, when living in a cold climate, I fear feeling trapped.

After the opening of "Archipelago," I contrast St. Thomas with New York City, the Voice of Innocence once again conveying factual images, what I—that young girl—observed at the actual time of the event. Next, through the Voice of Experience, the author "me" recasts these images metaphorically to show how I try to "carry" my island warmth and colors with me to the States.

In other words, the Voice of Innocence states what I see before me (the Marlboro Man, lights on a bridge, Horn & Hardart, chicken, apples, etc.); the Voice of Experience, meanwhile, conjures these items into the magic I actually felt at the time, but was too inchoate to express. The final paragraph of "Archipelago" is fully written in the Voice of Experience as I deepen the entirety of the experience by reflecting, finally understanding how, metaphorically, I've always carried the island with me, wherever I've traveled or lived.

This exploration is more interesting than the facts by themselves. We write creative nonfiction to discover the story behind the story—what we didn't understand or know at the time of the event.

As you write, pretend to toss a stone into a lake or river. Through the Voice of Innocence, write the compelling ripples of life you see on the skin of water. Then allow your gaze to follow the stone as it slowly sinks. Through the Voice of Experience, you'll discover what ebbs and flows below the surface as you peer into the metaphorical depth of you.

A FLASH NONFICTION EXERCISE

Step 1: Using the Voice of Innocence, describe one specific image of your childhood hometown. For example, you could begin by writing: *Walking to school during an ice storm, I slide from one sidewalk to the next.* This sentence conveys a straightforward rendition of what happened, typical of the Voice of Innocence.

Step 2: Next, using the Voice of Experience, continue to describe this wintry day in such a way that it metaphorically conveys how you feel about it, reflecting back, incorporating knowledge and language you lacked in the past. *Icicles spike down from rooftops and cover window panes like jail bars. When I walk to school during the storm, the air smells blank, scentless, as if the whole town is encased in ice. How will I be able to chip through winter and breathe, as I wait for spring?*

By using words such as "jail bars," "blank," "encased in ice," I show the reader what this town, and winter, felt like, what it meant to me. I am able, in short, through the Voice of Experience, to bring the reader inside my cold, icy world.

A FLASH NONFICTION ESSAY
Archipelago

When I'm thirteen, my family and I leave our home in the West Indies. On the day of our departure I pluck a red hibiscus, putting it in the pocket of my madras skirt. Now that I've finally absorbed the wealth of island colors, I don't want to leave. I lag behind my family as we walk from the tin-hangar airport, cross the tarmac, and climb into the sweltering cabin of the Caribair plane.

Even though I was young, in second grade, when we originally moved here from the States, my skin still remembers the chill of asphalt-gray mornings, frigid hands and feet. All winter, bleak trees longed for green. *I* longed. Static, as if suspended in ice, I waited to melt into spring.

Only here, on my island of mimosa charms and sunny amulets, I feel transfigured into endless days of warmth.

But the move is decided. My sister, now in high school, is too old to attend the Antilles School. She has to continue her education in the States. My father, a banker, secured a new position outside New York City.

After liftoff, I press my forehead against the window. I seem to see all my Caribbean life far below, in one glance, as we arc toward the horizon. For years, I walked up/down volcanic mountains, sandals slapping and scuffing Calypso rhythms. Our cook, Sylvanita, twisted chicken necks, voodooing them into dinner. I slept frothed in a mosquito net, stars and moon bluing the reflected viridian sea. I waded into dolphined waves, seaweed haloing my hair.

Now, the airplane itself seems gusted by trade winds, propellers spinning like silver doubloons through an operatic sunset—a chorus of ibis, bananaquits, blue-crowned euphonias. The sky is a blizzard of bougainvillea, poinsettias, flamboyants, before birthing an emerald-drop dusk, staining fields of sugarcane. Wanting to carry all of my green memories with me, I take a deep breath and strap my seat belt tighter across my stomach. I want to contain each ginger flower, each blade of fever grass. If only my suntanned skin would last all year long. Enough color, enough warmth... enough to last.

We land a few hours later, like magic, at Idlewild airport. On the way to the hotel, speeding across the city in a sun-yellow taxi cab, I press my face to the window. Times Square marquees blaze red and white, like neon frangipani petals, fluttering. Skyscrapers soar high as volcanic mountains. The Marlboro Man, tanned golden as a pirate, puffs halos of smoke—almost like my breath fogging the window. Rising above Riverside Drive, Yale Truck tires spin billboard lights, around and around, as our taxi crosses diamond-studded suspension, bridging water frozen by alchemy. Snowy clouds mystically cape stars and planets.

Later, when we leave the hotel, my new penny loafers strike steel-drum percussion on city streets. At Horn & Hardart, dinner is conjured behind little glass windows—an apparition right here at 182 Broadway. Roast chicken, seaweedy spinach, banana cream pie. Rich island-bean coffee pours from dolphin-head spouts. Here, a fistful of silver coins buys paradise, warm and perfect. Green and crimson apples glow as delicious as sunsets.

That first winter I barely feel the cold. Nor do I sense the wait-ing, month after month, for summer. Rather, I see warm tropical afterimages as if I only, just then, turned my head from the window of that airplane. For years, whenever I'm about to touch down in another port—no matter how far inland—I feel as if trade winds reverse, tugging me back. Always, at this moment, I see that long chain of islands I live in still… its outline, its history, its secrets of flaming abundance.

—Sue William Silverman, from Brevity

Barbara Hurd

THE SOUNDS AND SENSE OF SENTENCES

Aristotle maintains that, more than color or smell, rhythm and melody "resemble dispositions." It is musicality, in other words, that most strongly conveys sensibility, communicates emotional intelligence. If Aristotle is right, then we prose writers can enhance the effects of our writing by paying more attention to the sounds of our sentences. We can heighten the effectiveness of our sentences if we imagine writing not so much for readers but for listeners.

In this regard, prose writers have much to learn from poets, especially when it comes to rhythms. "If the rhythm falters," poet Michael Longley claims in the Summer 1999 issue of *Poetry Ireland Review*, "then the poem dies of heart failure." Reading good prose, we feel ourselves carried by patterns of sound and phrasing. The syntactic structure of the sentence should cause us to feel the same.

Sentence rhythms are controlled primarily by punctuation, patterns of accented and unaccented syllables, and sentence structures. Semicolons, obviously, slow us down, and dashes interrupt. A repeated pattern of iambs interspersed with dactyls can feel like dance moves, or tidal slosh in a marsh. The use and placement of short/long, dependent/independent phrases change the way we hear a sentence. Rhythms can hurl

Barbara Hurd is the author of three books of nonfiction, including *Walking the Wrack Line: On Tidal Shifts and What Remains* (2008), *Entering the Stone: On Caves and Feeling Through the Dark* (2003), a Library Journal Best Natural History Book of the Year, and *Stirring the Mud: On Swamps, Bogs, and Human Imagination*, a *Los Angeles Times* Best Book of 2001. Her essays have appeared in *Best American Essays*, *The Yale Review*, *The Georgia Review*, *Orion*, and *Audubon*, among others. The recipient of a 2002 NEA Fellowship for Creative Nonfiction, winner of the Sierra Club's National Nature Writing Award and three Pushcart Prizes, she teaches in the Stonecoast MFA program at the University of Southern Maine.

us from the beginning to end: "Wolverine tracks following caribou. It is a quick gait, a low-to-the-ground intensity. Five toes, claws exposed, heel pad predominant" (Terry Tempest Williams, *The Open Space of Democracy*). Or they can allow us to meander and glide: "Something told me that the child and its accouterments should have been left where the parents intended before they departed, left to the endless circling of the stars beyond the cavern mouth and the entering shaft of sun by day" (Loren Eiseley, *All the Strange Hours*). These tools at our disposal regulate and help refine the way a sentence or paragraph unfolds.

Though sonic pleasure matters, it isn't, finally, enough. Virginia Woolf, in *The Letters of Virginia Woolf, Volume III, 1923-1928*, says, "Style is a very simple matter: it is all rhythm. Once you get that, you can't use the wrong words." Well, maybe and maybe not. For some writers, rhythm may indeed precede words, but to say that the right rhythm leads almost unerringly to the right words seems naïve, or perhaps a symptom of living in a different time. Woolf, after all, never heard rap music or attended a poetry slam. But many of us have, and it's clear that there are many writers for whom rhythm alone finds the words, and the result is banality or nonsense, utterances devoid of complication—thoughtless, in fact. We all know how we cringe when we hear a thoughtless person speak. It isn't their rhythms that are careless, but the connections between their rhythms, their words, and their thinking.

Aristotle knew that when music satisfies, it's not just because we like how it sounds, but because it goes somewhere. Arrangements of phrasings and melodies take us from one place to another, so that by the end of a piano sonata, for example, we feel we've traversed some wordless gap, been pulled by the notes from incompleteness to resolution.

The music of a sentence, likewise, ought to do more than merely please the ear. It must please the mind as well. When a well-crafted sentence propels the writer (and reader) into the next sentence, it's because the dynamic among the various elements of a sentence—words, syntax, sound, texture, tempo, and rhythm—have a kind of forward motion. All these elements combine to give form and then movement to an embryonic idea until the shape and sounds of the sentence become a vehicle for consciousness.

The varied musicalities of sentences must, in other words, embody ideas. Consider, for example, a few sentences from Annie Dillard's *Pilgrim at Tinker Creek*:

> The moth's enormous wings are velveted in a rich, warm brown, and edged in bands of blue and pink delicate as a watercolor wash. A startling "eyespot," immense, and deep blue melding to an almost translucent yellow, luxuriates in the center of each hind wing. The effect is one of a masculine splendor foreign to the butterflies, a fragility unfurled to strength.

The description is lush, the sentences layered with phrases, the words often alliterative. The complex sentence structures echo the complexity not just of the moth, but also of the observer's reaction to it. Wonder, it seems, inspires a many-pronged attempt to get the description right.

But just a page later, she chooses a different kind of sentence to convey a different attitude. Describing a moth emerging from its cocoon inside a jar, she writes:

> He couldn't spread his wings. There was no room. The chemical that coated his wings like varnish, stiffening them permanently, dried, and hardened his wings as they were. He was a monster in a Mason jar.

Here, the sentences are simpler, the rhythm more abrupt, the verbs less vivid. The repetition of "wings" three times in such a short passage doesn't add musicality; it thuds, reminding us that this moth will never fly. Horror, it seems, calls for an unadorned statement of facts.

Poet Lawrence Raab, in in his poem "Letter," praises a particular sentence this way: "I liked its shape. I admired the way,/ young as you were, you could feel//one kind of thinking adjusting to another, one truth/ becoming a better truth." The narrator likes the *shape* of the sentence, which we understand as its rhythms and its interrogation of itself, its willingness to, phrase by phrase, fine tune its thinking.

Learning to listen to our prose, we begin to hear how sound can suggest the ensuing note/phrase, determine what idea needs to be varied next or sustained. A good sentence, then, becomes its own means of inquiry.

$\backsim\!\!\mathscr{M}\!\!\sim$

FLASH NONFICTION EXERCISES

1. From some of the great sentence-makers (Annie Dillard, Virginia
   Woolf, Loren Eiseley, or anyone whose sentences strike you as
   musical), copy your favorite sentences onto index cards and tape
   them around your house. Read them aloud, slowly and often.
   Then try imitating each of their rhythms and structures. Don't
   worry about modeling too closely; this is practice, not publication.
   Don't worry, either, about expanding beyond a single sentence.
   You're trying out something new, not trying to finish anything.

2. Experiment with sound rules: Write a 50-word sentence using at
   least fifteen words with, say, long "e" and/or "l" sounds. Compare
   that sentence to one full of short "u" and hard "g" sounds.

3. Try deliberately alternating long sentences with short ones. Listen
   for how the pattern does or does not propel the sentence sense
   forward.

4. See what happens when you write a string of five sentences, each
   of which begins with the same initial three words.

5. Read some of the great musical poets: Walt Whitman, Donald Justice, Pattiann Rogers, William Butler Yeats. Listen to how sounds
   roll into sound, down the page, to some satisfying resolution.

6. Write a sentence that you believe acts as a "vehicle for consciousness" and then write one that does not.

A FLASH NONFICTION ESSAY

Pauses

Silence, Cicero says, is "one of the great arts of conversation," but for
me, I confess, silence is sometimes less art, more evasion. Inside it,
I'm often cozying up to my own heart's soft spot, hiding in a pocket
of fog, or ignoring some reason to re-enter the fray, humming to myself the "shh-and-shh" that can also mean *there's no need to explain*,
which is the secret refuge of the self-indulgent shy one.

For years I've said I was a lover of small silences, those still spaces between missions—inter-missions, I might say—chances to defy the too-burdensome notion that all the world, and my involvement in it, is a-humming and ablaze. Years ago, in a crave-the-quiet phase, I heard the slap of waves on sand as ceaseless noise. In the woods, even the racket of oaks in autumn winds could rattle and disturb. Though less crazed these days, I remain alert to the glut of superfluous words. As a first-year pianist, I shrink from the barrage of sixteenth notes in two quick measures.

Back then, frozen lakes were a relief, as were the noiseless drifts along the hedgerows, error-concealing dabs of white-out, empty rooms, the rest notes, even now, in the peppered page of a scherzo score. The more pauses woven into the work I do, the more comfortable I feel. Is there something wrong with me, or are pauses some aspect of my sanity?

In music, a rest note can, by its command, make me lift my fingers. "Shh-and-shh," my piano teacher says as she counts out quarter-note rests, those squiggles on the score that look like weak-willed iron gates rethinking their prohibition to proceed. My hands hover over the keys; I listen as sound recedes; I'm poised and waiting.

Yes, wait, I tell myself, out of habit; for inside such possibilities might be the world in abeyance, the music both gone and still here. For my left hand: minor chords, and for the right: a melody and a blizzard of quarter-note rests like ghosts with a *cri de coeur*-half-thought of rising once again. Wait. Linger. No need to rush. These are not pauses that punish or harm.

"Go on," my teacher says. "Play them," she reminds me, "but don't stay there. They're rest notes, not graveyards."

But on the page, half-note rests do, in fact, sit like small tombstones on the ledger line. I used to hear a kind of refuge within them for the curled-up, inert, though lately, finally, something more: a pause with a pulse, full of longing and the insufficiency of words.

Beethoven's one of the culprits. Beneath his pauses lie a whole chorus of my desires and dissonance—the sorely needed next moment on hold, a tension that could either spring or sink me, until the music begins again, with even a single note, which might save the heart from becoming a bruised fist or its opposite: a shiny thing, full of foil and foolishness and the bright clang of noise.

Hearing all that, my teacher would likely stop me. "Tone it down," I can imagine her saying. "Such flourish merely marks the timidity you're feeling. Try it again." And I do, because a heart that invites its own rescue must, I tell myself, be engaged with others, even if that means interfered with, exposed. When I lower my fingers again, a tonic chord, heavy and full, closes one door and opens another. My hands on the keys have a new direction in mind, arpeggios to finesse, dissonance to resolve.

Sometimes now it seems they're everywhere, these pauses—pregnant, as they say—in things I never imagined: not just musical rest notes, but doldrums between dreams, shut-it-all-down blizzards, his silence, her silence, the angst of suspended beliefs.

I still love my hiding places, but they're more fraught these days with the desire that others enter them, more full of a heart on its way, now and then, to entering the fray of conversation in which lulls and interruptions might even be part of the art of thoughtfulness.

It's no longer just a need for small silences or a history of shyness, either, that makes me mindful of pauses, but the way they often arrive now, beckoned or not, helping me to hear what I've just done, readying me for what's to come. Maybe not intermissions after all, but improvised silences played below the surface, giving pause, so to speak, before they become those gifts worth waiting for.
—Barbara Hurd

Peggy Shumaker

LOCATION, LOCATION, LOCATION

When Judith Kitchen was putting together *Short Takes: Brief Encounters with Contemporary Nonfiction*, she asked me for a contribution. I had been working with brief pieces of prose for a few years, loving the elasticity of the form. As a poet, I paid close attention to how the rhythms of sentences differed from those of lines. I savored how I could play with sounds in brief prose, sending echoes through the piece to add emphasis and to alter pacing, to establish or shift tone, to add a formal moment or an element of surprise.

For that particular contribution, I wrote about 400 words set in childhood, 400 words at the edge of the arroyo that was the social center of my growing up.

After the fact, it occurred to me that this brief piece engages readers because they know where they are, even when the world of the essay comes apart.

The essay locates the reader in three essential ways:

- In geography (the edge of a dry river bed in Tucson, Arizona)

- In time (at the moment a flash flood crashes through)

- In character (the boy riding the flood/the children watching)

Peggy Shumaker served as Alaska State Writer Laureate from 2010 to 2012. She's the author of seven books of poetry, and her most recent collection is *Toucan Nest* (2013), poems set in Costa Rica. Her lyrical memoir, *Just Breathe Normally*, was published in 2009. Professor emerita at University of Alaska Fairbanks, Shumaker teaches in the Rainier Writing Workshop. She is founding editor of Boreal Books, publishers of fine art and literature from Alaska, and she edits the Alaska Literary Series at University of Alaska Press.

It's pretty hard for a reader to get lost when these three elements are clear. Once time, place, and character are established on the page, the reader has plenty to hang on to. The writer can compress the piece to its essence.

The first three paragraphs of "Moving Water, Tucson" let us know that it's summer in the desert, monsoon season. We find out that the dry arroyo is the gathering place for a gang of kids, curious and exploring. These children sense that their world is about to change—they can hear uncontrollable water not far off. The reader can take part in the deliciously forbidden moment of definite danger laced with irresistible curiosity.

These three paragraphs simultaneously draw us into a specific place and a specific moment of change. When a piece of writing does this, readers can dive in and make an emotional connection to the scene. Precise images (warm rain on our faces, tumbleweed, broken bottles) bring the physical world alive and suggest inner emotional worlds.

When somebody's teenaged brother decides to ride the flash flood, a character in action ups the emotional ante. A reader can feel concern: now a character is in danger, likely not to survive. The kids watching recognize both that the danger is real and that they want to be part of it. At first there's no discussion of this—just the torrent of language surging.

In the final paragraph, we get a notion of the relationship between the one who dares and those who watch him. The kid gets carried away, literally and figuratively. The very land we're standing on has shifted. The moment has changed everything. And the boy is still in the water.

Readers may not know that they have poetry inside them, in heartbeat and lung flutter, in brainwaves and blood rush. But they can feel the urgency when a kid is smashed against a bridge by floodwater. When the brown wall of water remakes the world, the language has to grow reckless and massive, has to surge and rush, destructive and all-absorbing.

In a very brief piece, we see characters in glimpses. The children watch, terrified and enthralled, as the older boy leaps into churning water. The boy riding the flood flashes by heroic and reckless, courting death while grabbing life.

The ending. Ah, the ending. Where is the end of a flash flood? Where is the end of childhood? Where is the end of a life? I chose deliberately to leave the scene unresolved. That's something you might try—make the decision to end your piece without resolving something important. See what that does to the energy in your writing.

↗

A FLASH NONFICTION EXERCISE

Read "Moving Water, Tucson."

Choose a place with special meaning for you, a place you can see clearly. It can be indoors or outdoors, a place you still visit or one you can't visit anymore.

Write a brief piece of prose using all three of these elements:

- specific setting (geography)
- moment of change (time)
- character in action (character)

Write a complete piece in 400 words.

For contrasting examples, you can use "Moving Water, Tucson" in tandem with Stuart Dybek's "Confession" (also in the *Short Takes* anthology). Dybek's essay puts us in the confessional at the moment the speaker realizes something unexpected about the priest—and about what happens during confession. The action is mostly internal, so writers can see that "action" and "change" can be internal as well as physical, and that "place" can be indoors as well as outside.

A FLASH NONFICTION ESSAY

Moving Water, Tucson

Thunderclouds gathered every afternoon during the monsoons. Warm rain felt good on faces lifted to lick water from the sky. We played outside, having sense enough to go out and revel in the rain. We savored the first cool hours since summer hit.

The arroyo behind our house trickled with moving water. Kids gathered to see what it might bring. Tumbleweed, spears of ocotillo, creosote, a doll's arm, some kid's fort. Broken bottles, a red sweater. Whatever was nailed down, torn loose.

We stood on edges of sand, waiting for brown walls of water. We could hear it, massive water, not far off. The whole desert might come apart at once, might send horny toads and Gila monsters swirling, wet nightmares clawing both banks of the worst they could imagine and then some.

Under sheet lightning cracking the sky, somebody's teenaged brother decided to ride the flash flood. He stood on wood in the bottom of the ditch, straddling the puny stream. "Get out, it's coming," kids yelled. "GET OUT," we yelled. The kid bent his knees, held out his arms.

Land turned liquid that fast, water yanked our feet, stole our thongs, pulled in the edges of the arroyo, dragged whole trees root wads and all along, battering rams thrust downstream, anything you left there gone, anything you meant to go back and get, history, water so high you couldn't touch bottom, water so fast you couldn't get out of it, water so huge the earth couldn't take it, water. We couldn't step back. We had to be there, to see for ourselves. Water in a place where water's always holy. Water remaking the world.

That kid on plywood, that kid waiting for the flood. He stood and the water lifted him. He stood, his eyes not seeing us. For a moment, we all wanted to be him, to be part of something so wet, so fast, so powerful, so much bigger than ourselves. That kid rode the flash flood inside us, the flash flood outside us. Artist unglued on a scrap of glued wood. For a few drenched seconds, he rode. The water took him, faster than you can believe. He kept his head up. Water you couldn't see through, water half dirt, water whirling hard. Heavy rain weighed down our clothes. We stepped closer to the crumbling shore, saw him downstream smash against the footbridge at the end of the block. Water held him there, rushing on.

—Peggy Shumaker, from *Short Takes:
Brief Encounters with Contemporary Nonfiction*

Eric LeMay

WORD HOARDS
On Diction and the Riches
of the English Language

Dictionaries lie.

Look at one and you get the impression that words line up like English school children, alphabetically, well-behaved, not one of them cracking gum or catcalling. But words aren't so orderly. Like wolves, they roam in packs; like hermits, they sequester themselves; like old tires, they roll through the language and land in places you'd never expect. And writing means working with words, not as *Webster's* would have them, but as they are: unwieldy, fecund, alive.

This essay offers one way of understanding how words work, especially for the flashier genres, in which you get so few. "Diction" is the critical term. It shares a root with "dictionary" and gets defined there as the "manner of expression in words; choice of words; wording." Diction shapes a work's tone and verbal texture. It's like the color palette and brushstrokes that compose a painting: Bruegel and Monet may both paint hayfields, but Monet's lush hues and hazy daubs differ vastly from the bold yellows and meticulous brushwork in Bruegel's harvest scenes. If *The Harvesters* and *Haystacks* were written instead of painted, we could describe these differences in terms of diction. I think of diction as the sorts of words we use and how we sort them.

For those of us writing in English, the sorts of words we use depend on the sorts of words that make up English, because English, especially American English, is a hodgepodge of words, mixed and mashed

Eric LeMay is the author of *Immortal Milk: Adventures in Cheese* (2010) and *The One in the Many* (2003). He serves as web editor for *Alimentum: The Literature of Food*. His work has appeared in *The Nation, The Harvard Review, Gastronomica, Poetry Daily*, and the *Best Food Writing* series. He teaches nonfiction writing at Ohio University.

together from the various languages it has encountered and absorbed, whether along trade routes, across battle lines, or through the doors of Ellis Island. English has Spanish words ("cockroach," "tornado," "ranch"), African words ("gumbo," "jazz," "juke"), Yiddish words ("nosh," "schlep," "smutch"), Japanese, Greek, and Native American words, Dutch, French, Italian, and Scandinavian words. The sorts go on and on. They make up the half-million or so words that fill English dictionaries.

Yet crack your *Webster*'s or *OED* and you'll see that, when it originated, English had two sorts of words. The first came from the Angles and the Saxons, those Germanic tribes who invaded the British Isles about sixteen hundred years ago and imposed their tongue on the isles' Gaelic-speaking natives. Their Germanic language became the first form of English, now referred to as Old English. The second sort came from Rome. About a century after the Anglo-Saxons conquered Britain, Pope Gregory the Great sent missionaries there to convert its inhabitants. Along with Christianity, they brought Latin and the Roman alphabet. Through their influence, English became a written as well as a spoken language, a wordy mix of the Latinate and Germanic.

My hipshot history misses most of what's fascinating about the origins of English, but even an initial glance at Germanic and Latinate words makes it possible to use the language more powerfully. To me, the two word-groups work like primary colors: You can paint with them or mix them to make other colors, but they also show how color itself works. Germanic and Latinate words reveal the nature of a writer's medium.

And they do so starkly. Compare the Germanic "thrill" to the Latinate "excitement." Or the Germanic "bad" to the Latinate "malignant." Compare "trick" with "illusion." "Dead" with "inanimate" or "deceased." These blatant differences in the feel of the language become more pronounced when you put them together. Here's a Germanic sentence: "Words of the same sort make for strong work." And a Latinate equivalent: "Vocabulary that possesses a similar nature results in effective prose." Same haystack, different paintings. The tone and texture change entirely depending on the sort of words you use, and these word-by-word differences add up, lending to the overall feel of a work.

Use, for example, a primarily Germanic diction, and your writing will tend toward the earthy and bodily. It will be direct, concrete, moored in time and space. Most of us lean toward these words for their power. The Germanic hews out raw feeling, makes stark what it describes. It's very show-don't-tell. When you use it, you draw your words from the hard core of the language.

If, however, you use a primarily Latinate diction, you'll get work that tends toward the abstract and cerebral, floating free of time and place. The Latinate limns thought. It appears in philosophical tracts, scientific research, those genres and modes that deal with complex ideas, often in specialized language. Latinates invite the mind into your writing.

Even so, many of us shy away from such words, since they can lead to vague abstractions, polysyllabic coagulations, and nominalized constructions (you see the problem). In this view, Latinates muddy a work's verbal surface and break the illusion that it's captured the world rather than artificially represented it. By calling attention to themselves, they supposedly ruin the *trompe l'oeil* that is the work.

While I'm sympathetic to this view, I don't share it. Avoiding Latinates may help apprentice writers who don't yet grasp how diction works, but it quickly becomes a minimalist straitjacket, a needless Oulipo constraint. Such work often cuts itself off from the intricacies that Latinates allow, and you'll struggle to reckon with subjects as complex as culture, morality, or mortality if you can only bleat Germanic words. Latinates unlock ideas, in part because they contain them. How much collective thinking already lies within such words as "culture" and "mortality," waiting for writers to build on or pull apart? An insistence on Germanic diction seems to me misguided. In principle, if not in practice, it chokes our linguistic resources before we start writing and so limits what our work can do.

In practice, of course, savvy writers have always mixed their dictions. Take this example from Julian Bell's *London Review of Books* discussion of a painting entitled *The Death of Empedocles* by the seventeenth-century Italian artist Salvator Rosa:

> The upright canvas, some 4'6" by 3', stood on Salvator Rosa's
> easel, prepared with a burnt umber ground. The painter first at-
> tacked it, as far as I can see, with a black-loaded brush, dragging
> a jagged stuttery line almost from top to bottom. That was to be

the rock edge of Etna's crater. Where the volcanic glow was to fall, Rosa slapped on a queasy mid-tone mix of sienna and smalt blue; capped it with brisk blurts of white; later, knocked the resulting rock planes back into readable order with red and yellow glazes. But that vertical divide of his, tumbling and forking in ever crazier lurches, still retains a lightning urgency. Here you meet the gestural painting of the 1660s, as vehement and imperious in its own way as the art of Clyfford Still.

It's not easy to make a description of a painting feel action-packed, much less heroic, but Bell does, largely because of his diction. He uses Germanic words to take what might seem a cerebral act, better fit for Latinates such as "cerebral," and turn it into a visceral one: His verbs ("stood," "see," "drag," "fall," "knock," "cap") give Rosa's painting vigor; his nouns ("ground," "top," "bottom," "rock," "edge," "glow," "blue," "white," "glaze,") give it substance; and even his modifiers ("upright," "burnt," "black," "loaded," "stuttery," "red," "yellow," "tumbling," "forking," "lightening") have a meaty vividness. Through Germanic words, Bell captures the rough physicality of Rosa's work.

He also interprets it. As the passage nears its conclusion, the Germanic diction that he uses to describe the painting gives way to a Latinate diction that explains its impact (the painting's "vertical divide . . . retains . . . urgency") and sums up its significance (an example of "vehement" and "imperious . . . gestural painting"). The Germanic may bring Rosa's painting to life, but the Latinate reveals that life's purpose.

This is how diction works: The words you use shape the writing you get, and being aware of your words *as words*—that is, as a medium with subtle variations in its nature and effects—helps you get the writing you want.

Yet using diction doesn't just open up how you might handle Germanic and Latinate words. It also highlights ways of working with more specific dictions, a possibility that takes us back to where we started: English is full of verbal groupings, large and small, that cluster around particular places and things, actions and ideas. It holds caches of words, bunches and bundles of words, what the Anglo-Saxons might have called "word hoards." Bell, for example, uses the diction of painting. His passage includes words involving a painter's materials ("canvas," "easel," "brush," "glaze"), a painting's form ("ground," "line," "plane," "vertical"), and paint's color ("black," "burnt umber," "mid-tone," "sienna," "smalt blue," "white," "red," "yellow"). He draws on these words—words that don't merely *refer* to painting, but that, within English writing, *are* painting—and they give his writing precision. His specific diction lets him paint nimbly on the page.

Bell's example leads to my final suggestion: Try sorting your words in light of your subject, because, whatever your subject, English has words specific to it, and they aren't always the ones that come most immediately to mind. (Our active vocabularies are always smaller than our passive.) To say it another way, the more useful question for a writer alive to the medium might not be "What am I writing about?" but "What am I writing with?"

∼

A FLASH NONFICTION EXERCISE

Create a piece from a specific diction. Usually, we begin writing in response to an idea or experience, but this exercise asks you to start with your medium: words. W.H. Auden once said you could spot a young poet if he or she liked to hang around with words and overhear them talking to one another, and this observation is true of most writers, whatever the genre, since words are all we have to work with. This exercise invites you to hang out with a particular group of words and listen to what they're saying, then craft a piece out of that conversation.

Begin by making a list of words about a particular subject. Words for mountain bikes or international treaties, words for welding or Lauren Bacall—it doesn't matter, so long as you're drawn to the subject. You'll want to read around, searching out specific verbs, nouns, and adjectives. You might look at Visuwords (www.visuwords.com), an online graphic dictionary that lets you explore the networks between words. Your aim is to create a word hoard: A group of words that conjures your subject matter in your medium.

Then work with those words to write your piece. Odds are, the words will work on you. Writers who try this exercise are usually surprised at the rich verbal textures they get, almost inevitably, because the list pushes them beyond the obvious words, the tired words, the magnetic-poetry-kit words that scuttle so much writing. The list becomes a micro-standard: The writing has to be as rich as the words from which it's made.

And this process isn't a matter of synonyms, like saying "orb" when you mean "circle" or "velvet" when you mean "cloth." That's a word-kit way of looking at the exercise. It's about precision, it's about energy, it's about the fact that some words have better conversations than others, and those conversations often happen, as they do for partygoers, when words share a common subject. Like carrots. My example comes from a list dropped through my mail slot. Whenever I flip through a seed catalog, I'm struck by how many kinds of carrots there are. Gradually, their names worked on me.

But those words make up only the most obvious diction in this piece. As you read, you'll spot others: Latinate, Germanic, even the homespun and the made-up.

A FLASH NONFICTION ESSAY
To Plant Twenty-One Kinds of Carrots, Probably More

> *The day is coming when a single carrot, freshly observed, will set off a revolution.*
>
> — *Paul Cezanne, in Joachim Gasquet's*
> Cezanne: A Memoir with Conversations

In the Ohio suburb where I grew up, tucked under the northern curve of Interstate 275, a carrot was a conical lump, rumpled and chemical-washed, less a beam of sunshine than a miniature traffic cone left in a ditch. A carrot lived in a plastic bag, at the bottom of the refrigerator, next to the anemic celery that my mother paired it with in side-salads: orange rounds scattered on iceberg lettuce. I'd hit them with blobs of blue cheese and work them with my molars. Usually, they'd splinter, though sometimes they'd send a jolt through my jaw hinge that would end in a boney thud just above my temples. "That," my father would explain, "is roughage." He'd then detail the benefits of roughage for what he called "regularity," as in "being regular" and "keeping regular." Where I grew up, a carrot was rough.

Not until decades later, and after I'd moved half a country away, would I come to see a carrot as a vegetable and, even then, I'd wonder whether it was really a carrot or some new hybrid, a cross between a beet and a carrot (a "beerrot") tricked out by geneticists with a love for Cezanne's colors. This carrot, spilling from a crate at the local farmers market in Cambridge, was deep purple, but, once bit open, had a center that ranged from orange cream to lemon zest. And it was sweet, eat-by-itself-sweet, with a hush of earthy spice. I pulled it from its bunch, greens still springing from its cap, and rubbed the dirt from its skin. It was called the "Dragon," a variety of carrot bred by John Navazio, a seed specialist who works to safeguard and develop organic vegetables and farming practices. I bought it for a buck.

I wouldn't immediately learn about experts like Navazio or the dangers of an industrial food production system like the one I grew up on, a system that relies on precariously few varieties that it breeds for yield and durability, but not flavor (not flavor!) or the preservation of our biotic heritage. That, too, would come later (often with exclamations). I did, however, start learning about carrots. The Dragon made me wonder if others were out there, obscured by that woody orange mouth-punisher I called "carrot." And there were: the Danvers and Paris Market, the Scarlet Nantes and St. Valery, the Sunshine Red, Little Finger, and Lunar White, the Oxheart, the Amsterdam Minicor, and the Autumn King, the Chantenay Royal and Red, the Amarillo, the Cosmic Purple, and the Tendersweet, the Imperator 58 and the Purple Haze, the Solar Yellow, the Red Samurai and the Atomic Red, which looks as though it's been basted with fire ants. I found these, sometimes at the market, but mostly as names. I'm sure there are more.

It's March now. Spring is almost here, and, after a recent move back to Ohio, I have the opportunity to plant a garden. The seed catalogues arrive. The earth softens and smells of must. I have an idea.

—Eric LeMay

Ira Sukrungruang

BYE-BYE, I, AND HELLO, YOU

I Am You, You Am I: The Disguised I

Much has been made about the role of the "I"—both positive and negative—in creative nonfiction. In memoir in particular, the "I" shifts from
the dynamic character-in-the-moment to the analytical writer-at-the-
desk. Sometimes unskilled usage of the "I" can lead to narcissism and
unneeded navel-gazing. Regardless, the "I" is essential in the essay. The
usage of this pronoun pronounces ownership, and it is this mode that is
the driving force in creative nonfiction; it is what makes creative nonfiction vulnerable, exposed, dangerous, and, I believe, quintessentially
unlike fiction and poetry. As Vivian Gornick says in the *Situation and the
Story*, there is no surrogate narrator, no stand-in; the "I" is a living breathing entity that exists in this world that s/he writes about.

But here is "What We're Good At" by Sheryl St. Germain. Here is this
marvelously short essay that does not use the "I," yet the "I" is ever-pres-
ent. St. Germain uses the second-person point of view instead of its sibling pronoun. The "you" is St. Germain herself, a woman who has just
finished making love, yet her mind is occupied with New Orleans and
Hurricane Katrina and her feelings of helplessness. This use of the second person is called the disguised "I." What the "you" does in St. Germain's essay is create this little pocket of intimacy, yet offers a necessary

Ira Sukrungruang is the author of the memoir *Talk Thai: The Adventures of Buddhist Boy*
(2010). His work has appeared in numerous journals, including *The Sun*, *Post Road*, and
North American Review. He has been the recipient of the New York Foundation of the
Arts Fellowship in Nonfiction Literature, the Arts & Letters Fellowship, and the Emerging
Writer Fellowship. He teaches at the University of South Florida and edits *Sweet: A Literary
Confection*.

distance for the writer. By taking away the "I" the focus shifts from St. Germain to the universal feeling of helplessness when faced with life's upheavals. This distance allows the writer to view the characters as characters without being emotionally swept away. The second person point of view allows readers to laugh at these awkward lines of dialogue, yet still feel the tension and darkness in them.

I Love You, My Friend: The Direct Address

There are other creative uses for the "you" as well.

My short essay "What If?" started when I received an email from my Polish friend after five years without any communication. *Yo, I'm in some shit and the cops are looking for me. I'm coming to stay at your crib for a couple of months. P.S. I love you.* He didn't sign his name, but his email address gave his identity away. I replied quickly—*Don't forget the guns!*

In the first draft of the essay, I used my friend's name. Instead of the direct-address "you," my friend was "he." After I completed the piece, the essay did not sit well with me. I read it out loud over and over—this is part of my process—and at the end of every reading, the essay seemed wrong. In fact, the reading made it worse.

The remedy came a couple of days later when I was teaching one of my favorite essays, "Tracks and Ties" by Andre Dubus III, in my beginning creative nonfiction class. I've been teaching the essay for years, and an incredibly compelling aspect of the piece is how Dubus addresses his dead friend. This direct address immediately makes the piece more intimate—something students will readily point out—but it also allows a deeper exploration of time and friendship. I asked my class, as I often do, "Why does Dubus use the 'you'?" And for the first time, a student offered this answer: "Well, if he used 'he,' it would sound like a eulogy."

There it was. The reason my essay seemed off—especially when read—was because it sounded like I was delivering a eulogy. I did not want to close the book on my friend, especially because he was alive and still wreaking havoc in Chicago. Although he is part of my past, he is part of the living and breathing past that I carry with me daily, a past that is alive with questions and complexities, a past that makes essay writing challenging and exciting. It was the simplest of fixes, the change of a pronoun, but the "he" presented a finality in the piece that was inauthentic to the relationship of these two Chicago boys, while the "you" seems to represent a continuity.

⁓

FLASH NONFICTION EXERCISES

Now it's your turn.

1. The disguised "I" assignment: Take an old essay you've put away and change all the instances of "I" into "you." Though this exercise is simple you may find that the simple change of the pronouns gives the essay a new life.

2. Write a letter to someone—someone close, someone important. Reminisce. Remember. See where the letter leads you. When you are finished with the letter, cut the salutation and closing. You may find that you have just written an essay of address.

TWO FLASH NONFICTION ESSAYS

What We're Good At

It is morning, winter solstice, the darkest day of the year, and you are lying with your boyfriend on his bed. You are from New Orleans, but you are now in Pittsburgh, where you came for a job and where you fell in love a few months ago. There is snow on the ground and it is cold outside. You have just made love, and you are happy, mostly, although there is a sadness in you that you doubt even the most wonderful lovemaking could dispel. You love this man very much, but your birth city has just been drowned, your brother is dead, your family displaced. It seems wrong to be in love when so much is the matter. You remind yourself that this is the first time you have been happy in love in a long time.

His hands roam your back, and you smell him everywhere, he is the air, and you breathe him in as deep as you can.

I fixed my vacuum cleaner yesterday, you say. He looks at you as if you are speaking a strange language.

Remember, it was broken? I took it apart and fixed it. A belt had come loose. He looks slightly confused. You suppose it doesn't seem like a thing of importance, certainly not something to bring up five minutes after making love. You are really thinking about New Orleans and how you cannot fix anything there, but you are talking about your vacuum cleaner. You hope he understands this.

I've had to learn to fix things, you say, *because no man I've been with has ever been good at fixing things.* You're not sure why you're telling him this. It sounds accusatory, though you don't mean it to be. It's a point of pride with you, that you can fix most things, that you don't need a man to do anything mechanical around the house.

He pulls back, his head on the pillow and looks at you. It's those dark eyes, Dutch and Frisian, that first cut into you, and still do. Those eyes want you to say the truth.

Even if you had offered, you say, *I wouldn't have let you fix it.*

At this point you think you should shut up because you feel like an idiot. You pull him close, feeling the warmth of his sturdy body, the sweet smell you love so much.

He is from a land that also lies beneath the sea, and his people are trying to help save your ruined city, but you don't know that they will. He has told you that the story of the little boy with his finger in the dike is a not true, just a stupid story Americans like to tell about the Dutch. And as much as he feels like a levee for your own rushing grief, you don't know that he can cure your sadness, which seems huge and gaping. What can love really do, you think to yourself, but do not say. You don't wish to hurt him. You love him. You want him to keep touching you, to keep saying he loves you. To keep putting his hands on whatever fractures there are in you.

I am good at opening jars, he says slowly, as if he is saying something monumental. *Any jar*, he says, *any jar that's hard to open.*

You feel like crying. He kisses you.

I'm also very good at pouring liquids from one container to another without spilling them, he says. This does not seem like such a useful thing, but you love him so you look in his eyes as if you understand why he is telling you this.

It comes from having worked in a darkroom for many years, having to pour things in the dark, he says. *Without seeing.*

Maybe, you think, it is a useful skill, to be able to measure things, to move confidently in the dark. You stroke the hairs on his chin. He continues.

I'm also good at getting keys out of cars when they're locked inside, he says.

You want to tell him that you are good at this, too, but it seems like the wrong thing to say. Instead you bury yourself in his arms and think of your family, your city, drowned and sick, so far away. You take deep breaths of his love.

At the moment you feel good at nothing.

—Sheryl St. Germain, from *Brevity*

What If?

—*for D.P.*

You had the habit of pulling practical jokes on me that pushed the line of decency: shooting BBs from your upstairs window like a sniper, wrapping my Jeep in industrial strength plastic wrap five inches thick, putting on a Halloween mask and stealthily breaking into my house and then standing over me with an air pistol aimed at my head while I slept.

This was fun for you.

Despite all of this, for a few years, you were all I had, and I liked your stories and I liked your pranks—though I would never tell you—and we were inseparable for a while, the muscled Pollack and chubby Oriental, two first generation kids making our way in Chicago, poking fun at other minorities in the confines of your Chevy Cavalier, the trailer trash car, you called it, with a web-cracked windshield and busted out lights.

"Dude," you said, pointing to the Hispanic man at the bus stop, "I think he's lost."

"Give him a map then," I said.

"Somebody should tell him Mexico is south from here."

"Check him for his green card."

"You got your green card?"

"This is America," I said. "Everything's green."

And you laughed like it was the funniest thing in the world before gunning the car to whatever destination we were heading to, the mall most likely, or Super Burrito.

Each night that summer, we found our way back to my house and we talked until you headed off to the graveyard shift at the lumberyard. You spoke of things I was not sure were true. That you sold coke and steroids at the gym. That your father was head of an underground crime family in Warsaw. That you had a candy bar named after you there. Mostly, you loved the "what if" game. What if we were gay? Who would we date? What if we committed suicide? How would we do it? What if one of us died? What would we steal from each other first?

The last month before I moved to Ohio, you spent most of the nights in the bathroom. I told you the new rule: Never shit in my house again. I told you something died in your ass. You laughed, but your face was wet with sweat and pale after you came out. You couldn't sit down. You lay on your stomach or leaned against the wall. One night, you asked me to come into the bathroom.

I didn't want to.

"I think something's wrong," you said.

You had been in the bathroom for over an hour and I was beginning to think that something was wrong. I walked in, covering my nose, spraying scented aerosol into the air. You pointed to the toilet. I looked and looked away. I wanted to see logs of shit or artistically chiseled poop. I expected you to laugh and tell me I was a dumbass for believing you.

But you didn't. Your finger remained pointed at the toilet. "It's been like this for a month."

"God," I said. "Flush. Wash your hands."

You did. And then in a quick move, you pushed me against the back wall of the bathroom and closed the door behind you. You sat in front of it and laughed long and hard as I pounded on the door and said I was in the epicenter of stink Hell. But I knew you wouldn't budge. I knew I would spend the night in the bathroom until my mother came home and let me out.

"Go see a doctor," I said.

"Yeah," you said and you sighed afterwards.

"What if your ass was a flower?" I said. "What would it be?"

"A dead one. One that attracts maggots."

"Go see a doctor," I said.

"Yeah." For the rest of the night, we chatted about the fragility of life, a deep and melodramatic conversation. The door stayed between us until you left for work, wedging my mother's golf bag under the knob.

The first night I was in Ohio, you called and said you were at a bar celebrating your disease. I could hear some boy band crowing in the background. "Crohn's," you said. "They have to take out some of my intestines next week."

"Excellent," I said. "When you die, I get your TV, right?"

"What a pal," you said. You said, "For you, anything."

—Ira Sukrungruang, from Brevity

Dinah Lenney

ALL ABOUT YOU

Okay: You've been warned about *you*—also "your," and "you're," and "yours," and "yourself." Especially because it's so easy to slip into second person without thinking about it (as a substitute for "one" or "they"), "you" can be tricky—seemingly sloppy and unintentionally confusing—and is therefore off-limits in composition classes, and scholarly essays, and most reportage.

But it wasn't off-limits for Carlos Fuentes, Marguerite Duras, Nathaniel Hawthorne, Samuel Beckett, Jhumpa Lahiri, Rumer Godden, Edwidge Danticat, Junot Diaz, Italo Calvino, William Faulkner, etc., etc., etc.—most famously perhaps, Jay McInerney—and no, you didn't just pull those names out of your hat (see how the *second*-person possessive redeems that cliché?), you're not that good; you found them on Wikipedia. *Gotta love Wikipedia*, you thought (though you're not about to admit it) as you scrolled down that long and impressive list.

And then you checked the definition, just to be clear:

> The Second Person Narrative is a narrative mode in which the protagonist or another main character is referred to by employment of second person personal pronouns and other kinds of addressing forms, for example the English second-person pronoun "you."

Dinah Lenney wrote *Bigger than Life: A Murder, a Memoir* (2007), and co-authored *Acting for Young Actors* (2006). Her essays have appeared in *Creative Nonfiction, The Kenyon Review Online, Water~Stone, Agni, The Los Angeles Times, The New York Times,* and elsewhere. She teaches in the Bennington Writing Seminars, the Rainer Writing Workshop, and the Master of Professional Writing program at the University of Southern California.

Well, all right, you can work with this, you suppose, although now you're loving Wiki just a bit less: Why so convoluted? And what's all this about *other* main characters and *other* addressing forms? But "you" it is, you're on board: Second person, to you, means "you." And though it's true that it can be difficult to sustain in longer essays, the second person is one surefire way, you're convinced, to get at the stuff of flash nonfiction. You want to reach a reader in just a few paragraphs? To enlist, endear, seduce, inspire, provoke, and collude? You hope to make him love you, want you, root for you in the space of a page and a half? And never mind *him.* Say a writer—that is, *you*—struggles to face off with (herself) *yourself* at your worst—your most awkward, embarrassed, or culpable: "I'm too old for that dress" reeks of self-pity; but "You're too old for that dress" is self-aware and self-deprecating. Or, on the other hand, maybe you can't figure out how to promote yourself at your best—your most intelligent, poised, and heroic—without sounding arrogant and deluded: "I'm a stunner in that dress" is obnoxious, whereas "you" in the place of "I" implies a sense of humor (at least you hope so). In either case, believe me (whoops), *you* is your very best friend. Think of yourself as "you" not "I" in short spaces and bursts (which you'll be able to control without sounding affected or precious), and things are bound to get interesting.

But why? And how? First, because, as noted, it's natural to fall into second—it's how we do in regular conversation (everybody, not just you); "You" is therefore friendly, generous, comfortable—it conspires and commiserates. Second, events and scenes thus rendered are all the more vivid and immediate for the reader *and* you.

And if you're too close to your subject? "You" allows you to take a step back; to watch yourself go through the motions in a way that is almost scientific, and that therefore precludes going-through-the-motions in the prose. Whereas if you're not close enough, "you" helps you to remember things you thought you forgot: Puts you back in the scene and allows you to recreate it in startling and original detail.

All this to suggest—and even insist—that second person allows and encourages you to cop to things you might otherwise leave out; to notice yourself within a larger frame; to be more observant and more understanding, perhaps, of the context in which you behaved as you did. Moreover, it slows down the pace of things so that the story happens to you and your reader at about the same time—both of you there, in the middle of whatever it is, however delightful or excruciating. Are there dangers? Why, yes—but the benefits outweigh the risks, which, per usual, are specific to the writer, depending on his or her individual strengths and weaknesses. Take you, for example: You tend to go on and on, not to be able to stop yourself once the case has been made. Which might be right about now, you think, though this has been fun—second person is fun!—but enough is enough, and back to work with you.

⌒℣⌒

A FLASH NONFICTION EXERCISE

Remember a time when you had to make a choice, any choice—what to wear, what to eat, where to go, whether to go, what to say, whether or not to speak up—no instance too big or too small, but best to focus on a time, or place, or thing that is significant to you, of course.

Or consider a rite of passage in your life, an event that changed you somehow.

Take on one or the other, the choice or the event (and maybe they are one and the same), and write an essay about it in the second person.

A FLASH NONFICTION ESSAY

Little Black Dress

Should you pack the dress? The little black dress? A sleeveless shift, darts at the bust, comes to just above the knee, meant to be worn with hose and heels, black on black, diamonds at the wrist, jewels dripping from the ears, lips lined in red, eyes lined in charcoal and heavily mascara-ed, the wand pulled through each lash real slow at the corners, the way you've been taught...

This dress—this is the dress that got you through—through and past and over the Opening, the Wrap, the Gala; that Christmas, that New Year's, that Black Tie event; a parade of your own anniversaries and birthdays, and everybody else's big one, besides. For this dress you bought a succession of pointy-toed pumps, pashminas, and push-up bras; it's this dress that gave the old Ford its cool (and the Dodge, and the minivan too in their day), that allowed you to descend from the passenger seat with a modicum of moxie, to give the Beast (you called it the Beast, big as it was, its ceiling rigged with popsicle sticks when it started to fall) to the valet at the Beverly Hills Hotel, the Bel Air, the Four Seasons, and even outside that gated monstrosity in Hancock Park, the pink stucco affair with the gargoyles on either side of the wrought iron gates across the driveway.

How many times in this dress, have you swung your legs—swathed in sheer Lycra with a seam up the back—around like a diver, to step from the car, to rise to almost six feet, to tower over the guy in the bow tie and vest in your three inch heels, to look down at him, all demure, all murmured thanks, when he called you Miss; as if you looked like a Miss, and as if you were driving a shiny new Jag—you wish—but you didn't look like you wished, not then, not yet.

O, you should be able to say when you bought this dress and what for... But you don't remember... That's the problem; the dress is that old—the seams beginning to loosen and disappear under the arms, the color fading there, too. Should you pack the dress? Should you ever wear the little black dress again? Should you?

You should buy a new dress, that's what you should do. And you've been dutifully folding down the corners in your catalogues, surfing the net, dropping over to Nordstrom's on weekday mornings, when the dressing rooms are empty, trying on dress after dress in three-way mirrors, under unforgiving fluorescent lights. Except. Except, this one has capped sleeves (unacceptable) and that one, an empire waist (flattering to whom?); not a garment can you find without lace at the hem (precious), a bow at the shoulder (puerile), gratuitous puckers, pleats, and pockets; all you want is a little black dress like the one you already have. Except, except...

When did it happen? When—how—did the lipstick get too dark, the eye-liner too severe? When, by the way, did people start telling you to color your hair? And when oh when did every occasion in the little black dress begin to feel just a little like Halloween?

So. Is it actually, finally time to retire the little black dress? You sit on the edge of the bed, the dress spread across your lap.

You remember a dinner party in Laurel Canyon. Back in the days when you needed a sitter. (That baby nearly grown now, has her own black dress, left it in the back of the closet when she went away to college this year; she didn't need it.) A party in a house on stilts; a woman there—a guest like you—petite and pale, boneless, with eczema on the fleshy backs of her arms, and yellow teeth, and halitosis. Somehow even so, she commandeered the evening, excluded you, it seemed, from every conversation, gazed at something just over your shoulder when you did speak, though she cultivated a special intimacy with everyone else at the table, even your husband, whom, you remember (how can you forget?) she invited to poker night the following week. Small and rubbery as she was, she slithered up close to him; to everyone but you, men and women alike— if they'd had awnings growing out of their eyebrows, she'd have been in the shade. You wondered, from exile, how they didn't back away from her, since you could smell her breath from where you were, though she said nothing directly to you all evening, not a word. Except. Except, "That's quite a dress," she hissed, not meeting your eye, as you passed each other in the hall, coming and going from the bathroom. You thanked her—you thanked her retreating back, that is—and she vaguely waved from over her shoulder.

You smooth the dress across your knees. You snap a thread hanging from the hem. Flick away a bit of lint near the neckline. You fold it in half lengthwise, lay it across the top of the suitcase, just so. You'll wear trousers, no doubt, with a silk and cashmere blend button-down cardigan, very appropriate. But—just in case—you're packing the little black dress.

—Dinah Lenney, from *Chaparral*

Norma Elia Cantú

WEAVING PAST, PRESENT, AND FUTURE IN FLASH NONFICTION

In grammatical studies, tense functions in a predictable fashion, and grammar books—from as far back as Antonio de Nebrija's 15th-century *Gramática de la lengua castellana*—have given writers much to work with as we conjugate verbs.

When we work as translators in a language not our own, however, the act of verb conjugation can become a nightmarish exercise that baffles and disturbs our sense of time. For a translator, tense is often a challenge, especially if translating to English from a language with a different temporal marker; even more challenging to translate are verbs conjugated to mark other elements than those found in English. But tense in our own language can present challenges as well, especially when we choose to tell a story that happened in the past and we slip into telling it in the present tense, or the historical present.

In flash nonfiction, tense functions as the skeleton whereupon everything hangs. Shifts in tense occur as do shifts in point of view for a variety of reasons. In my flash pieces, the shift often signals a movement in time through flashback or flash-forward all the while remaining in the present, or what I refer to as the "writing present." Especially in writ-

Norma Elia Cantú is a professor of English and U.S. Latina/o Literatures at the University of Texas at San Antonio. As editor of a book series, Rio Grande/Rio Bravo: Borderlands Culture and Tradition, at Texas A&M University Press, she promotes the publication of research on borderlands culture. She is the author of the award-winning *Canícula: Snapshots of a Girlhood en la Frontera* (1995), and co-editor of *Chicana Traditions: Continuity and Change* (2002), *Telling to Live: Latina Feminist Testimonios* (2001), *Dancing Across Borders: Danzas y Bailes Mexicanos* (2009), *Inside the Latin@ Experience: A Latin@ Studies Reader* (2010), and *El Mundo Zurdo: Selected Works from the Meetings of the Society for the Study of Gloria Anzaldúa 2007 & 2009* (2010).

ing creative nonfiction, or creative autobioethnography,[1] the shifts can be vertiginous for the reader. For this reason it is imperative that the writer know how to shift seamlessly and that the narrative remains firmly anchored to the story line regardless of where it may go—the past, the future, the present.

Discussions of tense often turn into discussions of point of view. In writing memoir, autobiography, or *testimonio*, as well as autobioethnography, the choice of point of view is limited to first person. Although using third person may work, it is not as immediate as the genres demand, and the standard advice in writing classes is to use first person and past tense. While this is good basic advice, it invariably results in predictable and occasionally stale prose. Various writers for blogs and craft websites will sometimes demand the use of past tense exclusively. Well, in my case, choosing a tense is more about the sound, the feel for the action—not what the editor requires.

But I do recognize that integrating various tenses into a piece must be done as carefully as darning a sock or patching up a tear. Although, of course, now with disposable clothing such skills have fallen by the way-side, but tense choice must feel natural and not disrupt the story. The reader must not be jarred or confused, but must move with the story to the past and then forward to the present and perhaps even have intimations of the future, all within the limits of a short flash piece where time is of the essence.

In nonfiction, the choices of using the third person or first person point of view as well as using present or past tense will result in the desired tone of the piece. A more distant, some would say, objective, tone is achieved with the use of the third person point of view and use of the past tense. However, if the goal is to engage the reader not so much in reflection but in an intimate and accessible tone, the choice would be present tense and first person point of view. If unsure as to which to use,

---

[1] A blended genre that takes the elements normally found in autobiography and ethnographic study, creative autobioethnography tells stories from a first person point of view; stories tend to be actual events told in retrospect and contain ethnographic data such as traditional cultural events (rituals, festivals, etc.), material culture (artifacts, objects, and the arts that produce these, i.e., quilting/quilts) and other traditional folk-life areas such as workplace folklore.

the author may want to test both and tell the story from various points of view and using different tenses. Ana Castillo's work of flash fiction, *Bocaditos: Flash Fictions*, uses the past tense and the present as she writes poignant tales. The successful choice ultimately is a matter of tone and what the author's goals are for the piece.

Writers of long memoirs or autobiography may choose the past tense since it is easier to sustain interest in telling a long narrative; yet, some writers are able to engage the reader with a tale told in the present tense. Frank McCourt's *Angela's Ashes* and Eva Hoffman's *Lost in Translation: A Life in a New Language* come to mind. Using the historical present is also advisable, as it allows the narrative to have the immediacy of the present tense and then shift to the past as the writer comments, reminisces, or muses on the action in the past. The present tense differs from the historical present in one significant way: the historical present tense suggests the past while the present tense is definitely indicating a present action. In narratives where the action happened in the past, but the author chooses to use the present historical, the reader may sense the author's desire to bring forth a sense of urgency or immediacy. In telling the same story in the present tense, the same sense of urgency may be achieved, but narrating the action using the present tense implies no knowledge of what is to come; it allows little room for foreshadowing, something that the use of historical present does.

While the past tense may be appropriate for all narratives of remembrance, it also may work well in historical fiction such as Emma Perez's *Forgetting the Alamo*, where the reader feels the immediacy of the action through the first person narration in the past tense. In this and other texts, the first person narration almost demands a past tense as the author is reminiscing. The past tense invokes a sense of analysis and reflection while the use of the historical present allows for a sense of urgency, similar to what we often hear on television newscasts with the use of the present tense. A newscaster may lead into a story saying, "Fire consumes apartment building," for example, about a fire that happened in the past. But what I find most compelling—although it is also tricky to pull off—is the blending of tenses.

In my autobioethnographic writing I often blend the tenses in a piece to take the narrative to the past and situate it as a NOW event. In the unpublished novel, *Cabañuelas*, for instance, I am remembering an event at a fiesta in Spain in the 1980s and comparing it to the next time I was at the fiesta in 2010. In this way, I can shift between what it was like 30 years before and how it is in 2010; but as I write about it from the vantage point of what I call "the writing present," the spring of 2011, I am allowed to insert a future tense as well. Here is the example:

> What I remember most about the first time I was at the Corpus Christi celebration in Toledo, Spain, in the 1980s, is the smell of thyme and rosemary, as the streets where the procession would pass were carpeted with the herbs. ... Last year, however, sprigs of thyme strewn on the streets did not offer the same intense odor; it was more subdued; it's the economy my friends joked, even the herbs are weak!
>
> At home in Laredo, getting ready to cook dinner, as I pull out the McCormick container the whiff of thyme transports me back to the streets of Toledo. In a few months, I will be back there once again. Will the smells of the fiesta welcome me back? Will I recognize the familiar sounds and smells? So much has changed, yet the fiesta remains the same: tapestries hung on the cathedral walls, children dressed for first communion offering flowers, the itinerant bands playing here and there, church bells ringing on the hour, and the city workers spreading thyme through the streets.

Of course the elusive nature of time means that the moment I write about a particular story, in this case of the Corpus Christi in Toledo, it is already in the past. As I am writing this sentence and situating it in the present, it is already becoming the past. As it becomes the past the positionality shifts immediately. That is the nature of time and writing within this time restriction—even as we live our lives—means that language must allow for the shift as well. Tense allows us to move in time and to reflect in writing what our lived experience confronts daily: a disorientation and a dislocation within time. Tense is a tool that we use to help us tell a story in time locations.

A FLASH NONFICTION PROMPT

Think of a photograph of yourself between the ages of five and 12. Answer the following questions as a form of prewriting:

Who is taking the photo? What is the occasion? What are you wearing? Be specific—color, fabric, style of dress, shoes. What is your hair like? What is on your feet? What are you sitting or standing on? What sounds can you hear? What odors surround you? If you could talk to the child that is you what would you say? If the child could talk to you what would s/he say?

Now do a 10-minute free-writing session, letting yourself go wherever the writing takes you, answering the prewriting questions or not.

Now write the piece in the past tense using the vantage point of today. You might want to begin, "I remember the photo of when I was…"

Now write the piece using the present tense: that is, in the first person point of view at the age the photo was taken. It might begin, "It is my fifth birthday party. I am standing outside our home and the odor of *carne asada* and the sound of *conjunto* from Dad's radio in the backyard envelop me."

Now write it as if you had just been born and you are telling the story in the future tense. "Five years later, I will be standing outside our home, and I will …"

Now work to weave the three tenses together from the vantage point of today, the writing present.

This option allows you to test out and then use the most effective tenses for the purposes of your piece.

A FLASH AUTOBIOETHNOGRAPHY ESSAY

Of Songs and Tears

Nena loved Judy Collins and every time she listened to her sing "Both Sides, Now," or "Clouds" as she thinks of it, she felt a tinge of regret, or maybe nostalgia; it was a feeling unlike any other that drew tears that she could not hold back. Sometimes she would get the same feeling at sunset, that time of in between, when it's not daylight anymore, and not quite night. Dusk. *El crepusculo. El ocaso.* But, there must be a word for the feeling in some other language, not in Spanish not in English and not in Spanglish. The Japanese had a word for it, *nuygen*, was that it? No. It didn't look right. She could never remember how to pronounce it, how to spell it in her alphabets. Had heard her Japanese roommate in Lincoln, Nebraska, say the word once and had made Amy—that was her "American name"—repeat it and write it down phonetically so Nena could remember how to pronounce it. But she had forgotten nonetheless, and the tears came nonetheless, no matter what the word for the feeling was. She wept. Cried in public, in private. Alone or in a crowd. Whenever she heard the song, the tears were sure to follow. "Clouds." One time she was in an elevator and the song came wafting in. No lyrics, just music and she wept. Elevator music made her cry! After that incident, she tried to purge herself of the feeling by playing the music over and over. She almost had it, too, but a few days later she was listening to an oldies station, as she drove to work. The song came on. Tears came as copious as ever.

Other songs also elicited tears. Chicano movement songs, *Yo soy Chicana tengo color...* instead of *yo soy rielera, tengo mi Juan....* all kinds of 60s and 70s songs that spoke her language, spoke of her dreams, her politics. Victor Jara singing "Te Recuerdo Amanda," Violeta Parra singing "Gracias a la Vida," she who had taken her own life. Mercedes Sosa. Suni Paz singing "Alfonsina y el mar" about the poet Alfonsina Storni, who walked into the ocean. Like Virginia Woolf. Peter, Paul and Mary's "If I Had a Hammer," "Leaving on a Jet Plane," "Puff the Magic Dragon," and Joan Baez songs that spoke to her politics. Old Mexican songs, the corridos that she had learned from her uncle. "Gabino Barrera," "Rosita Alvirez," and "El Caballo Blanco." Sometimes she sang at the top of her voice when she was cleaning the apartment. "Amazing Grace," "We Shall Overcome" ... So what if her voice wasn't really good, she knew all the words and after all had not Mr. Reyes in the penitentiary in Lincoln advised her, "*Vd. cante. Todo mundo sabe cantar, solo abra la boca y cante con el corazón y vera que se siente bonito.*" And she did sing and she did feel good. His songs also made her cry, but not always.

In Lincoln, she would go once a week to the penitentiary to translate for the inmates. After the work, Beto would take out his *tejano* button accordion wrapped in an old pillowcase, and Mr. Reyes would get his guitar and they would sing. Corridos. Rancheras. Tejano. Songs that made her homesick for South Texas. For home. The story was that Mr. Reyes killed the man who had killed his son. He was serving a life sentence for the murder, and according to Nena's friend, Betty, he had turned himself in, didn't regret the crime, he did what he had to do and that was that. Nena never asked what the men were in for. Unless it came up in the paperwork she translated for them, it didn't matter. When she came back to Texas, she missed the guys, their *relaje*, their jokes. Their music. Now in Spain, living so far away from Laredo, from Lincoln, she yearns for the soft sounds of their music. She listens to certain songs, Little Joe's "Las Nubes," Santana's jazz sounds, Lydia Mendoza's songs, music that reminds her of these men, and boys, trapped in an alien land in an alien place. Betty had written that one of the young guys had committed suicide and that Beto's parole had been denied once again. Lincoln was a world away. A world she no longer inhabited.

In Madrid, she doesn't have a record player; it is the time before digital music. No CD player, no CDs. Those will come in the future—when she visits in 2010, she'll have her pods in her ears, Buika's music softly playing, digitized. But back then, Nena misses the music that is always there in her home. So she listens to the radio. The Madrid stations offer a bit of everything—jazz, *sevillanas*, pop in English or Spanish and even French. Her favorite station's late night show comforts her. Every night, the host picks a theme and plays music from all traditions around that theme. One night, she tunes in, and there it is, Judy Collins singing "Both Sides, Now" and Nena weeps uncontrollably. What is the word for homesickness in Spanish? *Echar de menos.* To miss. In Portuguese it is more accurate, she thinks as she hugs her thin frame, wrapping her arms around herself. All the while she is weeping, her eyes puffing up. *Com saudades.* She whispers softly. When the tears come. She cannot stop them.

Paco comes into the room and holds her, *¿qué te pasa?* He whispers in her ear as she sobs like a child whose parents have left and she misses them so much it hurts.

Nada es la canción, this song always makes me cry. She lies.

—Norma Elia Cantú, from *Cabañuelas: A Love Story*

Aimee Nezhukumatathil

OVER THE RIVER AND THROUGH THE WOODS, TO ALMANAC WE GO

On the Use of Research and Lists in Flash Nonfiction

I love lists. I am a chronic list-maker: at any given time, one can find little scraps of paper along the borders of my desk where I've jotted various to-do lists, to-read lists, grocery lists, to-write lists—I even keep idea lists for birthday and Christmas gifts for my loved ones on a file on my home computer. And I love finding lists in stories, poems, and essays. There is much to be learned about a character or speaker by analyzing what he or she parses out in list form. What does he or she deem important or pressing? What rises to the top of one's consciousness and what echoes in the blank space between each item on the list? What gets lost in those small bits of radio silence?

And I confess, lists are one of the only ways I can write prose. As a poet, I find sustaining a narrative for any length of time (i.e., longer than a single page!) an extraordinarily difficult feat and am full of awe and admiration for those who do this on a regular basis. For me, even three finished pages is occasion for both agony and pride. *I know, I know.* But I'm so used to the compression, the telegraphing, and the clipped lines that poetry affords. And yet. And yet. I find that writing flash nonfiction by making lists of knowledge or observations gives a sheen and surprising depth to a subject that would otherwise take pages and pages of description to cover.

I like to think of writing flash nonfiction in this way as a kind of almanac-keeping. Almanacs are used to record occurrences in the natural

Aimee Nezhukumatathil is the author of three books, most recently, *Lucky Fish* (2011). Her poems and nonfiction have appeared in *Orion, Tin House,* and *American Poetry Review.* Awards for her writing include the Pushcart Prize and an NEA Fellowship in Poetry. She is an associate professor of English at SUNY-Fredonia.

world (tides, frost dates, rainfall, sunsets and sunrises, etc.) so one can prepare for the future. The tables and charts and lists are kept neat and tidy. There are no long, drawn-out descriptions of tornados or hurricanes, only when and where they occurred. No sensuous musings on moon-glow. Only that the moon did, in fact, wax and wane. Of course, writing flash nonfiction *too* much like an almanac would make for a rather sterile and tedious essay. But that's where you—the creative writer—step in.

Writing lists in this way may at first seem like you are writing *around* a subject; as if you are walking in circles in a forest, trying to find that clearing where you left your staked tent, the fire your companion started, the sizzling of roasted meats.

But keep at it. Separate each tidbit and step of knowledge or observation. Leave your reader with some white space and room to breathe and reflect between each morsel. When you telegraph or "kaleidoscope" your subject in this fashion, you will find surprise and recognition layered with new understandings and new renderings of the subject, so full of dark and good smells. By doing so, you'll be able to situate yourself (and the reader) without ever getting lost.

⌐≁⌐

A FLASH NONFICTION EXERCISE

Because the array of topics to write about can be dizzying for this form, and because the number one problem my students face when I give them a version of this assignment is some variation of, "But where do I *start?*" I'm narrowing it down to one exercise that still encompasses a wide range of possibilities, but will hopefully let you focus just enough to get writing:

Choose an element of nature that you are not familiar with—one that requires you to do some investigative reading and research.

In the example I include below, I selected the seemingly simple subject of dirt. State soils to be specific, because I was both charmed and delighted to find out that such a thing even exists alongside the more familiar state birds, trees, songs, flowers, and so forth. And I knew virtually nothing about soil, let alone the soil of my home state of New York.

So for starters, select one of the following: armadillos, Niagara Falls, narwhals, bee balm, jackfruit, cactus, The Grand Canyon, or pelicans. Or, simply choose an animal, plant, or landscape of your own preference. For the research part: investigate the zoology or botany of your subject. Field guides, almanacs, or encyclopedias are particularly useful in this regard. You might even be able to watch a video of your subject in action on the internet. In your notebook, jot down interesting facts or your own observations from life or from pictures/video you encounter. Select facts or observations in particular that seem like they could be cracked open with a few more imaginative lines. Divide each with white space, or a printer's symbol (those little designs such as an asterisk or hashtag [#] used in delineating writing sections). Then, the fun part: expand each fact just enough to create an original and surprising rendering of the subject at hand, and, with a keen eye and ear (and nose and mouth!) try to evoke a distinct mood.

All sections of your flash essay, despite any initial differences, should contribute to the overall subject the essay suggests, and the essay should not read simply like a collected and flat list of examples. For instance, in "The Soils I Have Eaten," I had hoped to evoke a sense of restlessness. The state soils I selected were all states that I actually lived in. Though I lived in Kansas for just under a year when I was 12, I always felt a sense of home and harmony in that state. (Little did I know the boy who would grow up to be my husband lived just an hour away from me at the time.) So for that state, that move in particular, I wanted to convey a sense of tranquility and peace.

Keep in mind, the whole of your essay—all the sections taken (read) together—should be greater than the sum of the parts. In other words, all of the "mini" essays together, as a whole, should read as a kind of metaphor, even going so far as to create a distinct mood or tone about the subject at hand. You'll find that even with a subject initially unfamiliar to you, a layered and richer understanding can arise through writing in list form. You'll be over the river and through the woods, so to speak—finding a clearing in your writing just when you least expect it.

A FLASH NONFICTION ESSAY

The Soils I Have Eaten

The state soil of New York is named for the place where a man lost his finger to a rattlesnake. The finger lays quiet in the ground. The snake's great-great-grandsnakes still chitter through this soil. Sometimes one snake gets the idea he can blink his eye. He concentrates on this single violet thought. A slick frog crunches a maple seed, and the snake immediately forgets what he was thinking.

~

Each bend of cypress root drinks a soft fen mud. Each beard dangling from a branch says: I am a dirty man who had soup for lunch. The state soil of Florida is Myakka—a fancy way of saying, S*and, sand, sand,* and if you dig further still? *Watery sand.*

~

Casa Grande is, of course, Arizona's state soil—salty and robin-red enough to make even the bottom of your pant legs blush. Dust devils whip against a flat house set against the side of Camelback Mountain. The camel's legs tuck up around palm tree and strip mall. He longs to eat a salad of thorn and dates. He longs to eat the leather of a saddle. If you squint, you can see the tongue clean his eye of gnats at night.

~

Harney sounds like a friend who will help you in a pinch: silty, loamy, good enough to feed your family, and mine too. In Kansas, we sit around the table and break bread with Harney soil. Good guy, that Harney.

~

In Illinois, I ate dark Drummer soil—mottled loam and gray clay. A little bit of city grit and soybean. A little light and dark. Street corner and silo.

~

Ohio's Miamian soil is like coffee at a dive bar: medium roast, hickory ash, a tiny dash of guitar and smoke. Where is the waitress with red stain on her cheeks, old phone numbers tucked into the ticket book at her hip? That used to be me. Where is the torn and pilled-up pool table, the dart board, the wall behind it pimpled with holes?

—Aimee Nezhukumatathil, from *Brevity*

Judith Kitchen

THE ART OF DIGRESSION

I'm the kind of person who can get things done. Who knows the most efficient route, or the best plan. Who does not waste time. This competency is good in life, but not so good in writing. In writing, I can defeat myself with my certainties. I can shut doors without even knowing they are there.

Digression has a bad rap. "Don't digress," people are always saying. "Get to the point," and, of course, the point of the essay is getting to the point, isn't it? And wouldn't that hold especially true for the short essay?

Like conversation, the essay is likely to veer away from its main point, to wander off, so to speak, into speculative territory. Essays are really an elaborate one-sided conversation, or so it seems to me. If you've ever said "Now, what was I talking about?" in the middle of a conversation, then you've been practicing the art of digression. On the other hand, there's nothing worse than someone who keeps saying "I want to get back to what I was talking about." (That's not the same as "I want to finish my story" because stories, obviously, need endings to *be* stories, but getting back to the "topic" was never in the contract for conversation, frustrating as that sometimes can be. In conversation, we always walk away with unfinished business.)

To digress: to stray from the subject, to turn aside, to move away from.

Judith Kitchen's latest book of essays is *Half in Shade* (2012). She has edited three collections of short nonfiction pieces for W. W. Norton: *In Short* (1996), *In Brief* (1999), and *Short Takes* (2005). Her awards include two Pushcart prizes in nonfiction, the S. Mariella Gable award for a novel, and an NEA fellowship in poetry. She lives in Port Townsend, Washington, and serves on the faculty of the Rainier Writing Workshop Low-Residency MFA at Pacific Lutheran University.

The concept of moving away, turning aside, is an important one. This is not quite the same thing as changing the subject, or moving toward something else. Instead it is a natural outflow of association, an aside that grows directly out of the material and builds until it has a life of its own—it is getting a bit lost on the way out in order to make discoveries on the way back. In following a spontaneous train of thought, the writer incorporates new strands into the text, and these provide new ways of looking at old material.

And, if the essay is a one-sided conversation, then reading an essay is also a one-sided conversation, and there's room for readerly digression as well. Far more than when we read poetry or fiction, where the author creates a context for us, in nonfiction we read with a kind of alternative reality in mind—our own. We move rapidly from the text to our own experience and back again, testing what is said against what we know, what is recounted against what we have experienced, what someone else thinks against what we think about the same subject.

In reading fiction, we willingly repress our own experience in favor of what is happening to the characters. We enter new worlds, and only if the author makes some glaring gaffe—cell phones in World War II, for example—do we step outside of the text in disbelief. The writer recedes, and only in retrospect do we even begin to address his or her world view, what he or she is trying to "say."

In nonfiction, since we are not—quite—tracking a narrative arc so much as a theoretical or philosophical one, we almost always try to figure out what the writer is trying to say. In doing so, we end up "taking off" from the essay at hand, reliving moments from our own lives, rephrasing our positions on issues, meandering into the world of our own thoughts even as we follow the course of someone else's thinking. The reading process is far more interactive, more like engaging in a discussion. This interactivity, I suspect, is because a major element in reading nonfiction is the assumption of the author's presence as a distinct character. Thus, in a sense, we read to digress—to argue and compare and extemporize—as much as we read to "get there." This dual nature of the "reading" is built into the genre, and writers of nonfiction need to understand how it works in order to take full advantage of it.

For the essayist, digression can serve many functions: first, it can add dimensions to what might otherwise be a simple statement or observation; second, it can help provide alternative perspectives, several directions from which to approach the same subject; third, it can provide pacing, deferring a moment of denouement, giving the reader time to catch up; fourth, used judiciously, it can leave room for readers to "enter" the piece by bringing experiences of their own to the discussion; fifth, digression can become its own method of making meaning.

The "art" part of digression knows how the new subject enhances the old, or when to return to the subject at hand. The opposite of this artfulness is what I will term "bad" digression, which unnerves the reader, gets in the way. In other words, digression that feels extraneous does not deepen or enlarge the piece.

My advice is to court digression. To court those places in the mind that we usually shut out because they would appear to lead us astray. Let your conversation get away from you; let a new story take over; follow a mental argument to where it begins to eddy in the current of its confusion. If something creeps in unnoticed or else pops instantly into your mind, don't put it aside in favor of where you already sense you are going. No, follow it up by—to use an expression common to those who work with horses—giving it its head. Something may happen along the way, something to alert you to its relevance. And then trust yourself to find the connective tissue—to make your new direction intersect with your old one. Trust me, the brain struggles to make sense of whatever is put in front of it. So how could you doubt that your brain will find ways to connect what you're thinking about now with what you were thinking about just a few minutes ago? Your brain will find some connection. Or, if not your brain, then your heart. There may be an emotional connection that defies logic.

So don't be too quick to scrap what occurs to you. There's time, later, to decide what's irrelevant. That's for revision, with its long, slow taking of stock. For the moment, you want more, not less: other forays away from the mainstream of your thoughts, other moments of digression that will begin to add up to something of their own—a weft across the warp of your initial premise. Suddenly you'll find yourself weaving that tight little potholder of your childhood, building a pattern of colors, an interesting texture. It's all there, waiting for you to learn how to finish the edges and, fresh from summer camp, hand it to your mother.

⌒ℳ⌒

A FLASH NONFICTION EXERCISE

Begin writing a scene that contains some description or action. Produce four to ten sentences, then stop.

This is your first paragraph.

At this point, the essay could go in many directions, depending on the type of digression. Try one version where the thoughts grow naturally out of what you have, but then take on a life of their own. A good way to do that is to use one of the following connective phrases to lead you into digression:

- That reminds me . . . (I am reminded of, this is reminiscent of, along those lines, etc.)

- I used to think . . . (That was before, I realize now, etc.)

- But it is also true … (Here is an alternative perspective.)

A second option would be to use the same first paragraph, then change the topic, maybe not entirely, but in some active way. Feel free to make an abrupt change, one the reader will intuitively understand.

Or, as a third possibility, use the same first paragraph, insert some white space, then write something that refers to one detail in that opening paragraph. This is a tangential digression and yet the two sections will inevitably be linked through this association of imagery or detail. Again, there will be a new dimension and a sense of depth. Often this type of digression is strengthened by doing it twice, producing a three-part piece, where the connections seem to multiply.

The essays, or beginnings of essays (all starting with the same paragraph), will take on distinctly different tones and engage decidedly different ideas, depending on how the mind departs from the original paragraph. But in each case, the digression moves the piece from mere anecdote into the territory of idea and the realm of emotion.

Now choose a title to round them off, a title that comes not from your initial idea, or your digression, but from the wedding of the two.

I've tackled the exercise myself, and the three brief essays that resulted are reproduced below.

FLASH NONFICTION ESSAYS

Time to Come In

All the neighborhood kids knew the calls: Steve's and Marilyn's father let out a sharp whistle between two fingers and they went running; Eleanor Tubbs could lift her voice over any baseball game; Gordie Mallett's mother's voice was too soft and she sent her equally quiet husband shuffling down the sidewalk looking for him; my mother's voice went up a notch and held onto its note until what you heard was mostly vowel riding the updraft. When she called us individually, we knew it was something specific, and usually some-thing to be suspicious of. *Judeeeee*. Or *Geoooooorge*. We knew we were in for it. But when she just wanted us both to come in—dinner, bath—she didn't think. *Joooordeeee* we'd hear sailing into the night, and we'd grin at each other because we knew we wouldn't go in, not until she corrected herself. Not until she remembered there were two of us.

Along those lines, all three of my grandsons' names end with an n. Benjamin, Simon, Ian, their vowels telling them apart. *Eh-ih, eye-oh, ee-ah*. I rarely mix them up, but then I am not distracted by dinner on the stove, or approaching bedtime.

Grandchildren allow a kind of time I don't remember having as a parent. Time to watch for incremental differences, and to savor all the moments stolen from routine. They run down the beach, and your eyes never leave the shape of their sturdy bodies. Your ears catch every nuance, "There's an ice cream store near here, you know." Grandparent time, I'd call it, like ferry time, when things stand still for a while and you live in the present. You live in a way you never remember living, and you realize that that is the gift they give to you, as you give them the undivided attention your mother never quite managed as she called you back to the fold.

A Kind of God

All the neighborhood kids knew the calls: Steve's and Marilyn's father let out a sharp whistle between two fingers and they went running; Eleanor Tubbs could lift her voice over any baseball game; Gordie Mallett's mother's voice was too soft and she sent her equally quiet husband shuffling down the sidewalk looking for him; my mother's voice went up a notch and held onto its note until what you heard was mostly vowel riding the updraft. When she called us individually, we knew it was something specific, and usually something to be suspicious of. *Judeeeee*. Or *Geoooooorge*. We knew we were in for it. But when she just wanted us both to come in—dinner, bath—she didn't think. *Joooordeeee* we'd hear sailing into the night, and we'd grin at each other because we knew we wouldn't go in, not until she corrected herself. Not until she remembered there were two of us.

My father didn't often call us in. But when he did, it was precise and no-nonsense. He had a curious authority. Oh, I remember the summer I was seven when he spanked me nearly every day until my mother reminded him that it clearly wasn't "taking." He must have found new methods because I don't remember being spanked after that. Yet I always knew what punishment would await me. How dire it would be if I crossed the railroad tracks in the middle of the block, without going to the crossing. How long I'd be sitting inside while the others were out playing if I did something like that. And I had no doubt that he would find out. He had scientific methods. On the other hand, he was the one who opened the skylight and let us climb out on the roof to play. And he was the one who encouraged climbing of trees and jumping into the lake and hammers and nails. With complete logic, he simply told me that "even though I was a girl" I could do those things.

Science, in our house, was a kind of god. Statistics ruled. So it didn't come as a surprise when I was headed to New York City after my sophomore year in college that my father ended an argument between my mother and me with an atlas. Still, just before his death, it did come as a surprise when he seemed to throw off his science in order to defend O.J. Simpson, so sure he'd been framed that he scoffed at DNA. And more of a surprise when he elected to have an operation that doctors told him was unlikely to succeed. We felt lucky, then, that his scientific self had written a Living Will, that when we were called on, we were able to hold out his science as a tenet of faith.

Night Calls

All the neighborhood kids knew the calls: Steve's and Marilyn's father let out a sharp whistle between two fingers and they went running; Eleanor Tubbs could lift her voice over any baseball game; Gordie Mallett's mother's voice was too soft and she sent her equally quiet husband shuffling down the sidewalk looking for him; my mother's voice went up a notch and held onto its note until what you heard was mostly vowel riding the updraft. When she called us individually, we knew it was something specific, and usually something to be suspicious of. *Judeeeee.* Or *Geoooooorge.* We knew we were in for it. But when she just wanted us both to come in—dinner, bath—she didn't think. *Joooordeeee* we'd hear sailing into the night, and we'd grin at each other because we knew we wouldn't go in, not until she corrected herself. Not until she remembered there were two of us.

~

The long held note of the coyotes. Where do they live? We see their lit eyes in the headlights as they slink past, two of them trotting into the darkness, making their way to someplace close by. Over, and over, they perforate the night. We know they are there, but where, in daylight, do they hunker down? The morning dogs do not suddenly bark; their owners sweep up the hill tethered to the leashes, and no one stops—looks around—fraught with the sense that coyotes are following. No one halts, listening for footfalls, listening for what might be breathing in the underbrush.

~

All night, the body rumbling through the dark, the locomotives of my childhood, *chuffa chuffa chuffa chuffa*, up and out of the valley, away, away, streaking past the sleeping village, its lone light prying open the darkness. Up and away, the dream of the child rising, too, following the tracks into what might never be known. *Chuffa, chuffa, chuffa, chuffa*, out into the places found in her books: Scotland, Brazil, moors, and a deep blue sea. Out into places that settle, like salt, into the blood. Recall them now, as the body hustles its air in and out, raise them up in memory: stone cottage huddled into the hillside, lone piper pumping air into air until the whole spit shivers under its plaintive wail; white walls shimmering under relentless sun, the *urubus*, strange, distant vultures, riding the thermals as though they were toying with air.

—Judith Kitchen

Maggie McKnight

BUILDING A FRAME, GIVING AN ESSAY A FORM

I've always been a person of few words, both in speaking and in writing, so flash nonfiction is a well-suited genre for me. I appreciate the compression and concision required by short pieces; though I wouldn't call it easy, this is a more natural format for me than one that requires lengthy description and fully fleshed-out narratives or ideas. I enjoy the process of cutting back, pruning a piece so that only the strongest and most fertile words and sentences remain, small twigs that leave the fully blossoming shape to suggestion.

In fact, for some of the same reasons, graphic nonfiction also suits me well: it shares, I believe, many of the qualities of flash nonfiction. Scott McCloud says in *Understanding Comics*, "The art of comics is as subtractive an art as it is additive." When I'm writing a graphic essay, rather than 250 or so words per page, I generally have to whittle it down to a maximum of five to ten sentences, none of which can be long or complex. So writing flash graphic nonfiction means that one entire essay may consist, as the example I provide here, of a total of fewer than 300 words, including dialogue bubbles and other text within the illustrations. The images, of course, do the work of filling in what the words leave out, which can almost feel like cheating: in writing prose, I sometimes struggle with description that becomes too list-like, and not life-like. But by adding images, I get to literally adhere to the cliché adage, *show don't tell*, freeing myself from the constraint of finding the exact right words to portray

Maggie McKnight has published graphic nonfiction in *The Iowa Review* and *Fourth Genre*, among other places, and has published prose nonfiction in *Brevity*. She has an MFA in nonfiction writing from the University of Iowa, and she lives in the United States with her wife, child, and cats.

certain details. (It's also possible, though, to "tell" with pictures instead of showing: a close-up of someone's crying face can be just as unsubtle as the words "she felt sad.")

Framing an essay by starting and ending in the same scene—and sometimes returning to it in the middle—is a common technique that I started using unconsciously, but I think it works as an intentional means to shape a brief narrative. Done well, framing can be an effective means to subtly reflect on the story you're telling, or to put that story in a larger context. Framing can also give an essay a shape and a feeling of closure, a sense that this is one complete story or idea rather than a random fragment floating aimlessly from my brain to the paper. And it lends itself particularly well to short pieces because it's a way of giving a compressed shape to something that might otherwise be hard to fit into fewer than a thousand words.

Here's McCloud again: "Closure is the phenomenon of observing the parts but perceiving the whole." He's talking about closure between two individual panels in a comic, but this idea can be applied more broadly, especially in flash writing where by nature the whole must be abbreviated. Using a frame can be one way of abbreviating what otherwise could take up pages and pages of text.

Sometimes I don't immediately know that I will be using framing in a particular essay, as with "France 1993," the example I include below. As a lesbian, a fair amount of my writing has focused on issues of sexual identity and gender expression, or related issues of social justice. One day I came across a journal and scrapbook from a trip I'd taken to France at age 16, a few years before I came out, when I was perhaps at the height of my heterosexual exploits. I decided to write a humorous and ultra-brief history of my dating life, starting with excerpts from the artifacts of my trip. As I wrote, I realized the whole thing would make more sense if I framed it with a present-day conversation with my partner, putting this story of my past into at least a little context of who I am now. The original outline for this essay had it running several pages longer, and included more examples from my past, but I came to realize those were unnecessarily weighing down a piece that I wanted to be short and funny.

This leads me to several asides about graphic nonfiction of any length.

Since "France 1993" is shooting for levity and humor, it doesn't necessarily pack a deep emotional wallop. However, I've found that the graphic form can be an especially effective medium when writing about difficult or traumatic events. We often expect "comics" to be, well, comic... but that expectation, coupled with the extreme spareness of text, can help reduce some of the maudlin quality that is often hard to avoid when writing in prose about, say, a loved one's illness or death or some misfortune of your own. In addition to graphic nonfiction greats Art Spiegelman, Alison Bechdel, and Marjane Satrapi, some others who do this well are Brian Fies, David Small, and Miriam Katin, writing respectively about a mother's cancer, the narrator's childhood cancer and unhappy family, and an escape from Nazi-occupied Hungary.

On the flip side, the graphic medium can give a writer a chance to use humor by making visual jokes and even inside jokes, sometimes portrayed in such fine detail that they work as background setting and might otherwise go unnoticed. Readers who look closely at the university campus on page three of "France" (which I realize probably only includes those reading this very explanation) might notice that the clock tower is showing two different times on the two visible faces. People who went to a certain West Coast public university might recognize this frequent occurrence, which was the butt of many a groan-inducing joke.

In writing graphic nonfiction, you can also experiment with page composition and panel design, both of which can affect compression and timing. The standard comic strip layout of similarly-sized panels, one after another, misses out on some of the unique opportunities presented by breaking out of text-only writing. Believe it or not, a fair amount of scholarship exists about graphic work; those who want to read more can look up McCloud, Dan Raeburn, and French authors Thierry Groensteen and Benoit Peeters, among others. One of the techniques I employ in "France," as a way of emphasizing the present-day frame, is the use of borderless panels. Borders help give a panel a sense of shape, much like framing does for an essay. Borderless panels, then, can evoke a timeless or unresolved feeling, which I use as a way of contextualizing the distinct story from my past in a more open-ended sense of the present. (See McCloud's *Understanding Comics* for more.) I also chose to use borderless panels to make the present-day frame stand apart from the narrative contained within the frame, highlighting the framing technique by visual means. In the last panel of the essay, I reverse this and use a black background, which necessitates a panel border, to give more of a sense of finality.

Framing can work for longer essays as well, of course. The longer the essay, the harder it will be to remember the beginning by the time the reader gets to the end; therefore it may be useful to return to the frame more often. In longer graphic essays, I also sometimes use multiple framing techniques, or a frame within a frame: in a ten-page graphic essay, for instance, I might have a framing scene that takes up the first and last pages, and then the eight pages in between may be framed by a different narrative moment altogether while jumping back in time to several other fragments and memories.

Even when we're writing text-only essays, we often incorporate the most minor of graphic elements by using extra white space (or an asterisk or other character) to signal a break or transition, which is one way to set the frame apart. In brief essays, white space will especially help keep transitional text to a minimum.

So, just as a comics panel border or an actual physical picture frame does the work of containing a drawing or piece of art and giving it a definite boundary, so can a written frame hold and shape a piece of writing, keeping it contained to a particular shape while giving it a sense of completion. These frames, usually narrative, can be fairly inconsequential—a minor conversation or even just a narration of a thought process—but can help add a layer of meaning to the "meat" of the essay, the part within the frame. And in the case of flash nonfiction, this framing can contain the writing at a particular length, giving a definite beginning and end, turning an anecdote into a discrete, complete essay.

A FLASH NONFICTION EXERCISE

This prompt can be used to write a piece of prose flash nonfiction or graphic flash nonfiction, but if you're even slightly inclined, I encourage you to experiment with the graphic form, even if you feel you have no artistic talent. (Visuals can be created by computer, by collage, by copying: you needn't be a skilled freehand drawer to write graphic nonfiction.)

Choose a single, fairly simple scene and use it as a frame for writing about an event or series of events of somewhat greater significance than the scene itself. You may find it easier to start by first deciding on the event(s) that will be inside the frame, and then choosing the framing scene. The framing scene could be a conversation, or a walk, or a particular event; the important parts are that a) it should not be too complex, since your writing about it will be relatively brief; and b) it should have a clear ending (or at least you should be able to write a clear ending for it). You have two possible approaches: write about the framing scene only to introduce the main topic and then again to close; or, start with the framing scene, then go back and forth between it and the main topic, returning to the frame for the ending.

A FLASH NONFICTION (GRAPHIC) ESSAY

FRANCE 1993

Kyle Minor

THE QUESTION OF WHERE WE BEGIN

We begin with the trouble, but where does the trouble begin? My uncle takes a pistol and blows his brains out.

Now we may proceed to the aftermath. The removal of the body. The cleanup. The reading of the will. The funeral in West Palm Beach, Florida. The woman he wanted to marry, taking the ring he gave her and putting it on her finger after the death.

But this beginning is not satisfactory. The mourners are now parsing their theories of why. Did you know that he was brain damaged after that city dump truck hit him 20 years ago? Look at his children grieving on the front pew of the funeral room. Why wouldn't they visit him except when they wanted his settlement money? Had his settlement money run out? And where is his ex-wife? Why couldn't she love him enough to stay with him (for better or for worse, right?)? Do you think it's true he was physically violent with her like she told the judge?

Now we're thinking the trouble doesn't begin with the big event. It's the grievance that led to the big event. Perhaps he wouldn't have killed himself if his children had more demonstrably loved him. Perhaps he wouldn't have killed himself if his wife hadn't left him.

Perhaps his wife wouldn't have left him if he had never been physically violent with her.

Perhaps he would never have been physically violent with her if his brain chemistry had not been altered by the city dump truck that hit

Kyle Minor is the author of *In the Devil's Territory* (2008), a collection of short fiction. His nonfiction, short and long, has appeared in Random House's *Twentysomething Essays by Twentysomething Writers*, *The Southern Review*, *Brevity*, *Best of the Web 2010*, *Gulf Coast*, and other journals and anthologies.

him 20 years earlier. So perhaps we begin at his house, in the morning, him buttoning his work shirt, smoothing the patch that bears his name on the pocket. Perhaps our story is about the workings of chance. What if he had stopped or not stopped this particular morning to get coffee? What if he had ordered two hash browns in the McDonald's drive thru instead of one hash brown, but had to wait a little longer for his order, since only one hash brown was ready, and the second hash brown was still in the fryer?

But this, chance, isn't story. Chance doesn't satisfy the itch story scratches, or not chance entirely. Story demands agency. But whose? My uncle was no dummy. Why was he a common laborer? Why didn't he go to college?

Now we're parsing family-of-origin stuff. His mother and father. My grandmother and grandfather. She was a lazyish homebody who wore a muumuu in her trailer every day of her life I knew her unless it was beauty shop day. He was a well point foreman who spent his child-raising years as an alcoholic who yanked the curtains off the walls. She didn't finish the eighth grade. He only finished the sixth. Maybe if she had thought school was important, my uncle might have gone to college, got a white collar job, missed the dump truck. Maybe if his father hadn't made my uncle sleep in the bathtub almost every night, my uncle might have been more alert in school, been encouraged by some teacher to go to college, got a white collar job, missed the dump truck, married a different woman, had different children, earned until he was eighty.

But what if his mother and father had never met and married at all? What if sperm and egg had never met? Or what if, as my grandmother once asserted, sex was not a nasty thing forced upon her in the night, but rather a thing of love and passion? Or what if something had been different in Owensboro, Kentucky, where they met in a roadhouse? What if the idea of love somehow transformed my grandfather into a man who could declare that for his seventeen-year-old bride and their children-to-be, he would never touch the bottle again? If we change a variable here and there, my uncle doesn't lock the doors, lie down on his bed, stick the pistol in his mouth, and blow his brains out.

And if we can lay some causal blame upon my grandparents, what about their parents? Who was this Kentucky coal miner Jess Westerfield who kept making babies with women and then making babies with their sisters? What did it mean for my grandmother, the little girl that she was, to sleep in winter on the floor of a drafty shack in the mountains near a clear cut someplace? Who were the men her stepmother aunt brought home at night after her mother died?

Again we enter into the questions of chance and existence. What if a mine collapsed upon Jess Westerfield before he could make his way from the bed of one sister to the bed of another? What if he mistimed a subterranean dynamite fuse and blew himself to death? What if there was a weakness in the rope that was used to lower his cage from the surface of the mountain to the mine shaft below? What if the rope snapped, and he was crushed among the others in the bent metal, or run through by some sharp stalagmite? No Jess Westerfield, no Wilma Williams. No Wilma Williams, no uncle. No uncle, no suicide.

Thinking this way, we're soon thrown upon the exigencies of history. What if that proto-Westerfield had not gotten on the boat from England and sailed somewhere toward the southern colonies? What if somebody a generation or two later had not heeded the call west, and settled in some Appalachian hollow and made somebody who would make somebody who would make Jess Westerfield, who would settle even farther west, in Owensboro?

What if the winds had not cooperated in 1588, and the English had not won the Battle of the Spanish Armada? Would anyone in North American be speaking anything but Spanish? Would anyone in England?

And what if the Taino Indians had known enough to find a way to kill the genocidal murderer Christopher Columbus in the year 1492? Would the continent have been overrun by Europeans?

And what if the Angles, Saxons, and Jutes had not imposed their barbaric Germanic languages upon the Celtic Britons at the point of the sword? And what if the Roman Empire had not grown fat and lazy and become overrun by Vandals? And what if, on some prehistoric plain somewhere, the people homo sapiens had not triumphed over their Neanderthal neighbors?

And now our trouble—the inciting incident of the story of my uncle's suicide—has moved past the historical and into the cosmological. It could be, as the ancient Finns say, that the world was formed from an egg that was broken. Or it could be, as goes the diver myth of the Iroquois, the earth was covered with muddy water at the beginning of time. When a Sky Woman fell from above, she was caught by water animals who made a home for her by diving into the seas to bring up mud, which they spread onto the back of Big Turtle, and this mud grew into the great landmass. For all I know, maybe the Incas were right when they spoke of an earth covered with darkness until the god Con Tiqui Viracocha emerged from the present-day Lake Titicaca to create the sun, the moon, and the stars, and to fashion human beings from rocks he flung toward every corner of the world, and he kept two of them, a man and a woman, by his side in the place they call the navel of the world.

But this of course is the story of my uncle, and if on his terms—a man who came of age in Florida in the 1960s—we're talking origins, we're talking either the Big Bang Theory, in which the universe began from some ultra-dense and ultra-hot state over 13 billion years ago, which predated the fabric of space and time and has continued to expand outward ever since, or, more likely, we're talking the literal rendering of the Book of Genesis he would have heard in the Southern Baptist church as a child: *In the beginning God created the heaven and the earth. And the earth was without form, and void; and darkness was upon the face of the deep. And the Spirit of God moved upon the face of the waters. And God said, Let there be light: and there was light. And God saw the light, that it was good: and God divided the light from the darkness. And God called the light Day, and the darkness he called Night. And the evening and the morning were the first day.*

By one way of thinking, we've entered into a cold intellectual exercise of technical cause-and-effect, which couldn't be any more distant from the story of a flesh-and-blood man who wore a mustache his entire adult life, who never felt comfortable in a suit, whose smile was crooked after the accident, whose voice was believed by his nephews to be unsettling and weird. We're laying blame and skipping all the important stuff, like how it seemed the last time we saw him that he was finally turning it around, that this woman he was with was a good thing. She was a jeweler. He had bought a house. Together they were buying a commercial building. You could see a future where she joined him on the cross-country road rally races he occasionally joined. In time you could see him becoming a man who didn't complain about losing the love of his ex-wife and his children every two or three hours. You could foresee a big-screen television in the living room, a big black leather sofa, satellite channels, the premium package with the college football games from the western states and Formula One auto racing from Europe and Brazil. You could see that the ring he had bought her would soon enough be on her finger where he wanted it instead of in her purse where she could think about it. You could see her negotiating with herself over time, talking herself into marrying him. That was why they were so often coming to visit my parents' house in the months before he died, no doubt about it. She was willing him a close-knit family so she could join it.

At the funeral, somebody said what always gets said, which is all things work together for good to them that love God, to them that are called according to his righteousness. And I wondered, if the story started there—because that's the classic "In the beginning" scenario—what did that say about a God with agency sufficient to create everything and set it into motion, and apathy enough to let it proceed as an atrocity parade?

Or what does it say about me, the god of this telling, that I have to take it there? Because it is within my power to do what I now want to do, which is to start the story with the more pleasing trouble Henry James prescribed—the trouble of he and she, and how they met, and how he toured her jewelry shop, and how she showed him how to shape a ring, set a precious stone, finish a setting, display the thing under glass, move a delicate hand in the direction of the display case, match a ring to a finger, watch a man and woman walk away wearing the symbols of their love. And couldn't I end it somewhere in the world of promise, he and she beside a lake somewhere, he opening the box, showing her the ring he had commissioned for her, he being sure to seek out the finest jewelry maker in town, knowing her discerning taste, and she saying she approved, the ring was lovely as the man is lovely, turning to him, kissing him, saying not today and not tomorrow, but there will come a day, I feel it, I believe it, something good is in our future?

◦*◦

A FLASH NONFICTION EXERCISE

Are you the teller of your tale, or is your tale the teller of you? Do you not have choices, even in a short piece of nonfiction writing? Isn't the question of where we begin only the first of a hundred technical choices that collectively determine how a piece of writing means or feels or exists as an object in the world? Is memory a simple dictation machine, or is it an active process to which attaches all of your intelligence, knowledge, speculation, and writerly (and humanly) know-how? Are you slave to a brief telling of scene followed by image or reflection, or are you slave to a summary of events? Or is every combinant, recombinant, reflective, analytical, moral, id-driven, and lyrical contortion available to you, as you attempt to understand a thing not in its simplicity, but in the complexity that vexed you enough to set fingers to keypad? Is what you're saying all that you have to say? Do you only think about what thoughts you think, or do you also think about what thoughts are thought by other people? Do you think your trouble is singularly a product of your own impulse toward trouble-finding, or do you think your trouble is the latest manifestation of a long parade of trouble that started marching, baton-twirling, and tuba-tooting long before anybody imagined there would ever be a you to name, and which will continue long after your bones mingle with all the other things under the earth the survivors dance upon? In rendering your story large, have you made the world that is its context too small?

Play with time—where we begin, where we end, the relationship between the time of the events and the time of the telling—is not the only technology available to you. Your job, this time, is to do as Jimmy Chen has done below, in his essay marking the aftermath of Hurricane Katrina, "The Water Is Rising Pleas," and find a form no one has ever found before, or appropriate a form from some other genre than flash nonfiction, and deploy it to ends no one has ever deployed it before.

Your subject is a given. It's burning a hole in you right now, and maybe you don't want to face it on the page. Sometime this evening you'll be lying in bed, not yet asleep, but not fully awake, either, and it will be gnawing at the edges of it. Be arbitrary. Make a form your subject—a structure built on time, a time built on a counting machine, the shape of a counting machine built on the vast swamp your great-grandparents crossed with two oxen and a wagon and a mule—and let your real subject ride your special way of counting or fill your shape. Consider that the trouble might not be what you think the trouble is, and the beginning you thought you wrote might not be the beginning, but the middle or end.

A FLASH NONFICTION ESSAY

The Water Is Rising Pleas

Put a grown man on his roof, put in his hand a house painter's brush and he'll paint these words for the helicopters to see. His friend lays asleep next to him, a water bottle in his hand. A damp American flag, shaped like koi, curls against the wind.

Open the door and the water comes out, gushing in its quest for equanimity. A woman in sandals braces herself, holding onto the metal banister. A tattoo, above her left ankle, is half erased from the years.

A chair in the middle of the street, legs up like a beetle. A rusty boat with children in it, their fathers nipple high in the water, pushing the boat towards its goal. Without any leaves, the trees are a Japanese ink wash.

The windows are broken and the drapes are sucked outside of the buildings, flapping like sad genitalia. A small wet dog in a garbage can, eyes over the rim. A man in yellow running pants stands on his mattress, legs braced, floating.

Man leaving his house, his clothes inside a plastic garbage bag. He makes waves that crest over the door knob, disappearing and appearing again.

Here! Mass 9:30 Bring Chair. The letters are spray-painted white. The church was leveled. The bishops, in full uniform, light candles and hold crosses. The choir behind them, wearing sunglasses, is bisected at the neck by the ocean. Their heads form a sort of mountain range, only less jagged.

Three sisters, a year apart each, pose for the camera. Their faces deformed by the rippled curling photograph that holds their frozen gaze.

Woman with her head swung back as if her spine dissolved, small eyes those crystal beads catch the light and melt down her cheeks. Palms together like she is washing her hands but she is not.

The helicopter blades are a blur, infinite moments stacked together into a fuzzy circle. Come down, come down and bring us up.

—Jimmy Chen, from *Brevity*

Nicole Walker

OF ARTIFACTS AND MRIs, OR STUCK ON THE WEB WITH YOU

Some people are inspired to write entire books by a singular experience with an object. Mark Kurlansky, in his book *Salt: A World History*, writes:

> I took [a rock of Catalonian salt] and kept it on a windowsill. One day it got rained on, and white salt crystals started appearing on the pink. My rock was starting to look like salt, which would ruin its mystique. So I rinsed off the crystals with water. Then I spent fifteen minutes patting the rock dry. By the next day it was sitting in a puddle of brine that had leached out of the rock. The sun hit the puddle of clear water. After a few hours, square white crystals began to appear in the puddle. Solar evaporation was turning brine into salt crystals.

Some people are naturally outward looking and go out of their way to find a subject that not only interests them but happens to have centuries-long history behind it. Others, like me, come across subjects by circumstance and surprising accident. While I was writing a piece about how, in order to eat the flesh of a dead animal, one needs to remove oneself—dissociate the pleading brown cow's eyes from the plastic-covered red meat of the grocery aisle—I was simultaneously taking my daughter to receive an MRI. How one sends one's kid through a machine that hurls magnetic rays at them, through them, takes as much ability to depersonalize, compartmentalize, to remove

Nicole Walker is the author of the nonfiction book *Quench Your Thirst with Salt*, which won the 2011 Zone 3 Creative Nonfiction Book Award and will be published in 2013, and a collection of poems, *This Noisy Egg* (2010). She edited, along with Margot Singer, *Bending Genre: Essays on Nonfiction*, which will be released in 2013. She currently teaches at Northern Arizona University's MFA program.

oneself as it does to eat the flesh of a doe-eyed cow. But also, what do I know about MRIs? What do I know about dead cows for that matter? While exploring the world of MRIs, I happened upon the world of cows. Or was it the other way around? It is in the cross between writing about what I think is my subject and exploring around that I find my real subject.

I get stuck a lot when I'm writing. I write on my computer, which is dangerously connected to the Internet—letting me out of me and out of the stuck I'm writing in—which makes me feel like I'm writing when I'm actually searching Google.

I follow one Boolean search to the next. I'll be typing along in Word, riffing in some way on the lexical beauties of encephalopathy and I wonder how exactly do I pronounce that so I wander out to the Internet and look up encephalopathy but I become distracted by bovine spongiform encephalopathy. This of course makes me think of steak, which simultaneously makes me hungry and a bit grossed out. I toy with images in my mind, toggling back and forth between sautéed mushrooms accompanying a rare steak and a cow's eye I saw once while I was walking alongside the interstate in Loa, Utah. The cow wanted me to pet it but I know nothing about petting cows and what that would do to the relationship between the cow, the steak, and me. I probably should have petted that cow. It would have been a kind of research.

I conduct research but not the research of hypothesis and argument. Often, it's a random kind of researching hoping to catapult me into finding a subject or thinking about my subject in a new context. I've sat in on classes outside of my discipline and incorporated the topic and the vocabulary from the discussions into my essays. I've attended a turkey race and an ice-sculpting festival, and used Wikipedia and randomly clicked until I found something I'd never heard of but was compelled to read about anyway. Research gives the piece worldliness, breadth, and perspective. This kind of research isn't the planned, methodical kind that books like *Salt* require. It's a different kind of deliberation. It's the kind Thoreau claims when he leaves for Walden:

> I went to the woods because I wished to live deliberately, to front only the essential facts of life, and see if I could not learn what it

had to teach, and not, when I came to die, to discover that I had not lived.

This is the kind of research that suggests the writer must go into the wilderness to look for something to see.

Creative nonfiction is a place to explore. Although it draws from elements of every genre, its ties to traditional forms are lax. Whereas I inhabit my poems, in nonfiction I sleep somewhere *out there*. Writing poems is an adventure of mountaineering. The precipices are steep and the toeholds few, but the ropes are strong and the path is tested. Creative nonfiction, as old as the essay, always seems new because who knows what you're going to find out there. It's a bit like *Survivorman*. The spontaneity of unplanned research and the associations made between that research and the circumstance I find myself in are freeing. It is a luxurious place where I rely on techniques from across genre—the character development and narrative arc from fiction, the leaps made of white space, the obsessive image in poetry. And yet I have to claim neither narrative nor lyrical—I am wandering in the woods. The form I use is the path I design myself.

As the writing gets closer and closer to revealing something the writer is not quite prepared to see, and therefore to say, the sentences spiral, the paragraphs break, the writer (dissociated even here as I think of watching myself write) changes the subject as fast as she can. I go to the computer for another idea. It's disturbing how very human the cow's eye is. I wonder how the cow's brain images magnetically. The ideas attract.

It's in the looking away that I look to something else. Then I look back again. That yoking together of seemingly disjointed elements surprises. In moving back and forth, the cow and the MRI reveal their likeness to me. The resonance between their likenesses moves into and becomes the voice. That resonant voice opens the research like so much simple harmonic motion and finds connections where no one would have thought to look. As Thoreau says "It's not what you look at that matters, it's what you see."

A FLASH NONFICTION EXERCISE

How to see something unique, different, idiosyncratic—how do you make your brain do it? How do you transfer that looking to the page?

The idiosyncratic moment is the thing that elevates personal narrative to essay. You can find it by research, you can find it by obsession, or you can find it by two conflicting stories fighting or supporting each other.

How do you take the reader beyond story and into something less transient, more textured, more layered?

By weaving two narratives together, you can sometimes find tangents and hidden meanings and tease them out to make a larger point.

Your assignment is to think of two unique stories. Start telling a story of you in a particular situation, as unique a situation as you can remember, where you were somewhere uncomfortable and had to figure out what you were doing there, what your role was. Put your body in a place. Depict as much scene as you can. When you get stuck or pause for a moment, start over with an entirely different story, a more personal story, something that you think you've known for a long time. As you develop the story, figure out if there's information that you're missing. That if you got something wrong, the whole story would change.

Threading two narratives together in this way might work for you as it does for me—giving me a broader canvas onto which to figure out what I'm trying to say.

A FLASH NONFICTION ESSAY

Dissociation (The Natural Order)

As if thinking the worst will stave it off. As if making a list of bad, worse, and worst will in some way hedge your superlative bets against the poles of news. I'm interested in the politics of thought. In the methodology behind wishing. In figuring out how to go against nature. In figuring out how to let nature run its course. The difference between right thought and right action.

~

There is chicken on the bone. There is chicken off the bone. Chicken on the bone is all the chicken I'd want in all its decadent renderings—by all I mean one. Fried chicken. There are many bone-in chicken recipes, such as chicken hind-quarters in port and cream, barbecued chicken, buffalo wings, though they too may be a kind of fried. But fried chicken is a testament to the beauty of the disarticulated chicken. Every piece a handhold. Every piece its own integrity. The coating wraps a thigh like snow, a breast like scarf, a leg like stocking to protect it from the cruel world of hot oil. Frying chicken is the nicest thing you can do to a dead chicken.

~

But there are some who cannot eat the chicken on the bone. Breast of chicken, boneless thighs, cubed in Korma, rolled cordon bleu, that's doable. At the bar, spicy drummette in my right hand, hot sauce on my cheek, a pile of bones in front of me, I turn to Alex who will not eat the boney chicken but is currently eating chicken tenders and I do not comprehend his reluctance.

"It's the same thing," I argue.

"It's not." He pushes my plate of sticky bones further away.

"But you eat meat. Chicken. Steak," I say.

"I prefer hamburger," he says.

Perhaps he does not like the resistance of muscle.

~

Hamburger is muscle turned to vegetable. You don't want to think muscle. You want to chew very little. You want to swallow before you can think about the sad heifer eyes. In the face of the accusing animal, you can solidly deny you knew what you were doing.

But what's worse? Finding joy in licking the rib clean? Of polishing the bone? Or letting the process happen behind closed doors for you by a grinder, a man in a once-white apron, by knives and forks not your own. You brought only your mouth to the table but it masticates to the same beat as mine.

~

I stream bad thoughts. I put through my head images of my hip blown open by a landmine. I am in the middle of Tooele near the

Dugway Proving Grounds, having driven toward Wendover, Nevada
for some very smoky gambling and returned without refilling the
tank, walking toward what looked like civilization but was really
anti-civilization and flagging down a security guard who was really
full-ARMY and not able to disclose that the most direct route to
him and to the gasoline that would get my car going again was a
hopscotch of landmines. When it erupted and metal showed off the
flag-like borders of red against white—my hip, at least, is patriotic—
I could speculate, it doesn't hurt so badly. What are these people crying so much about? Didn't you always want to see what the inside of
a chicken looked like anyway?

To avoid pity. To stave off self-pity. Here's the method: think the
worst first.

~

There are many degrees of vegetarian: from no meat can ever
have touched that pan to a little chicken broth won't kill me. The
first kind of vegetarian matches up nicely with the carnivore who
avoids bone. The second kind I can invite to dinner.

~

When Zoe is scheduled for an MRI, I stop talking to her. She's one
and a half and doesn't talk to me much anyway but usually, when
I'm changing her diaper, I tell her about the hawk that sometimes
sits in the tree outside her window. It's one of the first words she's
learned to say. At one and a half, she should be able to say something like two hundred words. Maybe even to make a sentence,
"there hawk" or "hawk flies." I used to tell her, between pointing out
her elbows and her knees, about the time there were so few hawks
that the squirrels overran the park, that even the dogs were scared to
run loose for fear the squirrels would gang up on them and attack.
I used to tell her, in between talking to her about the zipper on her
sleeper and the buttons on her shirt, about how a chemical they
sprayed to keep mosquitoes to a minimum ended up poisoning the
hawks too. I told her, between trying to convince her to say the "k"
sound of sock rather than just "saw, saw, saw," that now the birds are
back and so are the mosquitoes. I used to tell her, between buckling

her shoe and picking her up to look outside for the red-tail, that now
the mosquitoes will probably bring us down with their West Nile
or the hawks themselves will bring us the avian flu and topple us
quicker than any invading army. I used to tell her about the way an
owl can turn his head almost all the way around, the way the pere-
grine falcon flies as fast as a cheetah can run, that the big brown girl
hawk in that tree is being chased by the smaller boy hawk because
he loves her but they'll never be together because he's red and she's
all brown and they just don't match, a lot like her socks.

But I can't say any of this—even look her in the eye. It's better this
way, I figure, if she is already lost to me. If I am already lost to her. If
this magnet determines that her brain is neither human nor mine
we will have to move to isolate poles where the only bird that will
trouble her will be the penguin and the only bird to trouble me will
be regret. So I button her shirt and smile but I cannot bring myself
to say a word.

~

Is it necessary that the food I love most in the world be the most
inhumanely prepared? Does it follow necessarily? Does cruelty taste
good? Or is it the way we don't think about it? I see a flock of geese
fly over my head as we're driving by the manufactured pond and
they honk and I wave and I point them out to Zoe, to whom I can
speak again because the results of the MRI must be normal. The
word "normal" puts words back in my mouth. I say, "geese." I say,
"goose." I do not say, "*foie gras.*" Like all animal parts we eat, in preparing them, you destroy them. If you don't prepare it right, you can
ruin it. It's a fine line and many of those lines are the veins you have
to slide out from among that bulged out, fattened liver. To cut the
two lobes, you have to be quick with the knife. If you cut too slowly
or the kitchen turns too warm, the liver can turn into pure liquid.
The liquid cannot be made back into a solid. Once you've turned the
goose inside out, you cannot re-stuff him. You have to work quickly
and use a sharp knife, not only to kill but to cut. To de-vein. You
must use a sharp knife to separate the part from the whole even after the liver has been cut from muscle and ligament and artery and

skin. Cutting *foie gras* takes as much care as crossing a minefield. Like any minefield, one false move, and all that's left is blood and veins and solids seeping into your cutting board.

But if you cut it right, slice it fast, make your careful moves as careful as stitches, you can slice the *foie gras* into perfect rounds. You can sear it in a white-hot pan. You can top it with a sauce of wild cherry and *demi glace*. You can eat it. You don't have to think about it.

~

When she wakes up from the MRI, she seems the same as she did going in. The little cottonballs over her eyes are still taped on. There is more tape holding in the earplugs. Tape on her arm in case she needed an IV, which she didn't. The brain highlighted just fine. Her dad and I watch her lying there. She is like a mummy, ancient, wrapped. The veins run across her forehead like a map. If only the doctor could have read that cartography rather than the less visible map of the frontal lobe that the MRI has detonated in her head.

I am told to get the nurse when she starts to wake up. The minute Zoe moves, I want to go to her and pick her up and take her away from the people who discriminate against big heads and babies who say "hawk" both for bird and sky and sometimes chicken, but I do what I'm told and go get the nurse. She comes in with rubbing alcohol. She runs her fingernail under the tape, moistens the glue a bit, pulls a bit more tape back. This will take hours, I think. It's more important that we go home, I think.

I go up to the baby. I put my dirty, alcohol free finger under the tape and pull it off. Quick. Like a band-aid. She cries. To hear her resist, to come back into full voice, fills me with a little bit of joy. I pull the other five strips off fast. My method is painful but quick and I can pull Zoe up now from behind the white sheets and take off the pulse-oximeter and put her in her shoes and let her walk out the door.

~

Instead of going home, which we were told to do, we defy the doctors. Zoe is walking fine and she hasn't eaten since the previous evening and it's four-thirty now and what a better time for dinner at Rose's.

We look at the menu and although there are several good vegetarian options—pizza with goat cheese, portabella sandwich, fettuccine alfredo—what I really want is some meat. I order a steak. Rare. Cold in the center. I want to feel the smooth pain of the cow who suffered quickly with the bolt through his head. I make myself think of the bolt as it explodes into the cow's brain. I think of it and make myself eat a bite of meat. We don't have the results yet and it's time to face the facts. The brain may be faulty. The method may be cruel but the answers are abundant—I will force myself to think of it and do it anyway. I will take her to the machine that tosses magnets at her brain. I will pour the medicine down her throat while she cries. I will hold her legs apart and keep her arms wide for the x-ray like so much chicken. I will eat the steak and think of the cow's eyes and I will say the words hydroencephalopathy while looking at my daughter and pass a glass of water for her to hold between her little hands and tell her to drink carefully as if spilling cold water on her pants could hurt her. She drinks the water, compliantly, carefully. We're all walking on eggshells here.

The food comes. We've ordered chicken tenders for Zoe. She'll have to wait to get a little older before she can practice any cruelty by ordering for herself. I try not to think about it.

—Nicole Walker, from *Agni Online*

Jenny Boully

ON BEGINNINGS AND ENDINGS

To begin is to admit an infatuation, a longing, a love.

A beginning signals that one has moved well past being merely interested and is now immersed in what is most likely an obsession. To begin connotes more than falling in love: to begin is to commit, to stay, to hold.

To write is to encounter a love affair. And, as we groom ourselves and struggle to appear our most attractive to our beloveds, so too do we, as writers, want to present ourselves to our readers at our very best.

Or perhaps we get caught unawares: our ragged, disheveled, unsure, untidy, and ugly selves are what make someone else *love us*, for in writing there is always, inevitably, the ugly.

Love, in writing, is mostly a one-sided love.

Either I love or you love.

And, sometimes—although this is quite rare—we love each other. That is what makes the reader flip the page, that is, read past the *beginning*.

I am thinking about a beginning that I love, that I adore. I remember, always, so dearly, the beginning of Henry Miller's *Tropic of Cancer*: "I am living in the Villa Borghese." I will always remember "I am living in the Villa Borghese" and the rest of the first page and a half of *Tropic of Cancer*. My teenage marginalia reads, not naively, "This is the most beautiful

Jenny Boully is the author of *The Body: An Essay* (2007), *[one love affair]** (2006), *The Book of Beginnings and Endings* (2007), *not merely because of the unknown that was stalking towards them* (2011), and *of the mismatched teacups, of the single-serving spoon* (2012). Born in Thailand and reared in Texas, she has studied at Hollins University, the University of Notre Dame, and has a Ph.D. in English from the Graduate Center of the City University of New York. She teaches poetry and nonfiction writing at Columbia College Chicago.

beginning to a book. Ever." This is something I still believe today. It *is* the most beautiful beginning to a book. Ever.

I adore beginnings.

I adore the beginnings of love affairs.

When I teach a creative writing course, I oftentimes photocopy the first pages of books that I adore. I ask my students to guess the writers, the books. They are often wrong. Not only are they unable to identify a writer or book, they often cannot identify the genre.

The uneasy transmission of genre tells me a lot about the nature of love: spontaneous, unplanned, risky, and, yes, that most beautiful of writerly and loverly attributes: suicidal. For to write and to love, and to write and to love sincerely, is to write and to love like a kamikaze.

I loved the GRE Subject Test in Literature because I was asked to match first lines of literature to their authors and books. I, too, often guessed incorrectly, but I enjoyed so deeply the thrill of matchmaking.

However much I love beginnings, I know that eventually, I must write about endings.

I fear endings with the same intensity that I adore beginnings.

The fear is not the opposite, nor the negation of adoration; it is an altogether different sort of trepidation, for love is nothing if it is not trepidation.

An ending tumbles toward you over and over again; an ending will not stay flat, will not stay put; an ending troubles and taunts; an ending is sleep lost.

An ending is a puzzle without a picture; an ending says that there is no more to be done because, despite whatever it is that one of us wanted, nothing more can be done.

The doctor tells the family of the dying patient: there is nothing more to be done.

An ending tugs and tugs and tugs.

The beginning does not want the ending; the beginning, like so many young people, believes itself to be immortal, trusts the illusory material of existence and trusts that the distant point in the future that is ever-so-distant will continue to remain ever-so-distant. The ending is composed of distance and illusion; that is why the beginning, having not gone through the middle, believes that it too will live forever.

But we know, despite the feelings that a writer possesses upon writing a beginning, that endings happen, that beginnings do indeed come to an end. The book spine betrays; the word count is a demise, each page number an x-ing out of calendar days.

An ending is when a leaving leaves.

A beginning is asking: more please.

A beginning, in asking for more please, steps into that nebulous, often forgetful amnesiatic land of the middle.

The middle is the leaving.

The middle is ever-so-full of things that we did together as lovers that matter to no one else but one of us. For the middle is the story of love unrequited.

And so, an ending is when a leaving leaves.

When even the leaving has left you, then there is ever-so-much white space, I mean, an emptiness that tugs you to read the ending once more, to read the beginning again.

An ending says, I might have loved you once, but things have changed between us, things are different now. An ending says, it's not you, it's me.

Someone has moved on.

Someone has lost his heartbeat.

When I began to write *The Book of Beginnings and Endings*, I felt that beginnings and endings were *true*, that is, that the middle was nonsensical: the middle was all but a dream. A beginning stabbed like bright light, sharp stars. An ending lived inside me forever and forever; an ending was played out over and over again until it took on the shape of mourning, and then an ending was mourned until I felt that I could approach a beginning again.

The Book of Beginnings and Endings is just that: it is a book of solely beginnings and endings to hypothetical books. The beginnings end abruptly; the endings begin in the middle of things. It was my book about how love is always only a beginning and an ending.

The middles were only about the despair of the endings: the approaching ending and the ending of beginnings.

The importance of the beginning is to make possible the love affair; the importance of the ending is to make impossible the love affair.

The ending says, there is nothing else that I can do to keep you, and so—despite the heaviness and the utter heartbreak that you may feel—I leave you with such a small message, such a small sorrow, such a small sound. That is what an ending should do.

⌒⁂⌒

A FLASH NONFICTION EXERCISE

Go to an actual brick-and-mortar bookstore or a library and browse books in several sections that you would not normally. The more old books you encounter, the better your exercise will be. You may want, then, to visit a used bookstore or perhaps a library that has extensive holdings. Pay close attention to presentation, terminology, diction, and tone. How is the writing different from the literature that you encounter normally? Now, think about modeling your writing on one of the books from your excursion but using your own material. For example, how might you write about losing your grandmother's broach in the guise of a gardening text? Or how might you write about having lost a loved one in the guise of a sailing book? Now craft a beginning but only a beginning. Write a page or a few paragraphs and then stop. Or, give yourself a word count and then stop. Do the same with an ending. You might want to explore beginning in the middle of sentence or thought to see what effect that has. While trying out different voices, think about how you capture your reader and how you let your reader go.

A FLASH NONFICTION ESSAY
Strange Mechanism for a Dream

The decoder ring spelled out *forbearance*. If I wanted this, then I wanted this *last week*. Doctors have a way of making you believe that everything *will be okay*; thus, doctors have a way of making you *love them*. In the dream, the doctor held the instrument that listens to life against my heart. I sent a telegraph to a cloud and out came a thousand souls. The telegraph said: *forbear*. You may not know this, because you probably have never had to know, but I know it be-

cause whatever it is that I am doing, I am always interested in something *else*. (When you dream of a telegraph, it means that you are
not about to receive, but will deliver an important message soon.)
When a star "dies," it still exists; it is only said to "die" because it no
longer gives light. So too do I wonder about our living selves: do we
begin then, sometime, much later, to give off light? The star still exists; some stars, such as quasars and pulsars will continue to give off
signals, such colossal amplitudes of last life, a life line showing up
on no screen, continuously beeping for a celestial doctor who does
not come. Some "dead" stars, like black holes, we know exist simply
because of the behavior of other bodies around them; their gravi-
tational forces continue to attract whatever happens to live near
enough to be propelled closer to them. (So too do I behave in such
a way that suggests that someone I loved once still exists?) What the
unsuspecting body does not know: once there is a pull of attraction,
there is no departing, no leaving, and thus one gets crushed into
a cesspool so astoundingly dark and heavy that not even light can
escape. The star chart spelled out *forbearance*. In the dream, there
was an astrolabe that continued to point the way. (Strange that in
dreams there exist some machines that cannot be, or would not be,
used while we are our wakeful selves.) I used a strange mechanism,

~

Epilogue

instead of begloom, when real happiness, with real bliss, when I
point to a sunset and say something about *awe*.

Square No. 479

How is it that seasons change? Do they change so slowly so creep-
ingly because we so rarely break away from whatever it was that we
were dreaming to notice? What the season brings us to suffer (because seasons, no matter how lovely, will bring us to suffer) it brings
when we are not looking. I know the look of a cracked landscape,
winter in black and white, flat and finite with a sunset on the horizon like a red heartbeat suffering there. It will take me longer each

morning now to go out and face it, the leaves shivering then falling about as if to remind that somehow despite leaving, there is some magic, some beauty there. I don't want it: the mountain view, the shimmer of summer rain, a troutfilled creek. How is it that I came to be here this way with the wind a suggestion that it was, *indubitably was*, autumn (already and again)? What I want was in bed; he kissed me and said goodbye. And already, at three o'clock in the afternoon, the world takes on a stormy look.

Square No. 480

I know the forest creatures are in hiding from some great, unknown terror, a creature which is, in actuality, a mere shadow. I too go into hiding at the suggestion of darkness, of plot, of fullness. (Do you know what happens before arriving here? The *hyacinths* really are just *hyacinths*; the color of the sky, really, is not the shade of blue you'd like it to be.) I know the strangeness of animals that know only light and dark, sleeping and waking. The hand that cuts you free from the cloth is not necessarily the hand that sews you back in. I too have a scissors aimed at the sky; I too will slice open the belly of a great heaving.

—Jenny Boully, from *The Book of Beginnings and Endings*

Patrick Madden

WRITING THE BRIEF CONTRARY ESSAY

By nature and by training I am a mild contrarian, eager to doubt any bold pronouncement that comes at me detached from evidence or experience. This inclination has led me to my abiding fondness for reading and writing essays, a pursuit I sometimes accomplish in few words, in bursts of image, scene, or detail, but also at times in dense meditations on the intricate complexities of the world. To this latter category, the meditative essay, I will dedicate my thoughts here, in part due to my aforementioned peaceful subversive streak. I find so much of flash nonfiction to be populated by narrative and description that I want to open up some space for things philosophical, to think about thinking, even in its briefest forms.

From its inception in the 16th-century writings of Michel de Montaigne, the essay, from the verb "to attempt," has defined itself against genre expectations. In its very essence, the essay is a kind of anti-genre—not methodical, not linearly rhetorical, not narrative, not artful—and yet it is all of these things, in subtle ways. In his essay "Of Experience," Montaigne declares one of his guiding principles, that, "Ordinarily I find subject for doubt in what the commentary has not deigned to touch on," a statement that I take to indicate the Father of the Form's dissatisfaction with received notions and ready-made answers—his allergy to cliché, if you will. So the essay, during subsequent centuries, has continued

Patrick Madden is the author of *Quotidiana* (2010), a collection of personal essays, some of which have appeared in *The Iowa Review, Fourth Genre,* and *Hotel Amerika,* as well as in *Best American Spiritual Writing* and *Best Creative Nonfiction.* His second book, *Fisica Sublime,* is forthcoming. Since receiving his Ph.D. in Creative Nonfiction from Ohio University in 2004, he has taught in the MFA program at Brigham Young University, and has recently begun teaching at Vermont College. He manages the website www.quotidiana.org, an anthology of classical essays and contemporary essay resources.

this charge of revising understanding, re-seeing the familiar, re-thinking the taken-for-granted. It's no wonder that William Hazlitt, in his essay "On the Love of Life," stated, "It is our intention, in the course of these papers, occasionally to expose certain vulgar errors, which have crept into our reasonings on men and manners."

Ideally, then, an essayist has the sense to rise above pettiness and tribal politics. She thinks deeply about life, hesitates before committing to an ideology, undercuts and revises her own assumptions as she writes. "It is often the case," writes Phillip Lopate, introducing *The Art of the Personal Essay*, "that personal essayists intentionally go against the grain of popular opinion." They are interested less in what happened than in what it might mean, especially if the meaning seems fresh, contrary to expectations, new in connection or perspective. There's little to say in affirmation of the truths that everyone believes, but some small self-implicating excursion into divergent waters might open the author's and the reader's minds alike.

This is not to say that brief essays should look like the op-ed pages or sound like the television and radio news pundits' rants. In fact, while each may share some underlying dissatisfaction with the status quo, the essayist goes about her subversions in an introspective, self-doubting way, while the non-essayist tends to speak from a position of certainty, a hierarchical, patriarchal assumption that he has something to teach (and we'd better learn it). "Unproblematically self-assured, self-contained, self-satisfied types will not make good essayists," advises Lopate, no doubt envisioning some of our cultural pontificators.

Yet, despite all cautions, essays often do contain some moral rhetorical quality that threatens to improve not only their authors. In "She: Portrait of the Essay as a Warm Body," Cynthia Ozick, without abandoning her own stances, celebrates the temporary truces formed by writers willing to think against themselves. "By [the essay's] 'power,'" she says, "I mean precisely the capacity to do what force always does: coerce assent. Never mind that the shape and inclination of any essay is against coercion or suasion, or that the essay neither proposes nor purposes to get us to think like its author—at least not overtly." Which is to say that essays might not ultimately lead the writer and the reader to a simple inversion of a cliché, or to any truer version of a saying, but they are content with complicating, with requiring thinking beyond a bare acceptance of handed-down wisdom. In fact, some of the most pleasant contrary essays do not argue gravely with the great moral questions but toy humorously with platitudes whose validity is suspect, as will be seen with Charles Lamb's "flash nonfiction" in the exercise following.

Even in flashes (call them "flashes of insight"), then, we may find occasion to reveal the wanderings of our minds, the circumvolutions of comprehension that lead us to better (more complex, humble, nuanced) understanding. Of key importance in the writing of any essay, long or short, is the undidactic process of self-discovery. As Montaigne said, advising a widow "Of the Education of Children," "I aim here only at revealing myself, who will perhaps be different tomorrow, if I learn something new which changes me. I have no authority to be believed, nor do I want it, feeling myself too ill-instructed to instruct others." I, too, am of a mind to challenge my evolving assumptions in quick forays of contrary essaying.

⌁

A FLASH NONFICTION EXERCISE

Following in the venerable tradition of essayistic subversion, we will model a flash essay after Charles Lamb's "Popular Fallacies." First published in *London Magazine* in 1826, these are a series of brief contentions against proverbs of his day. Some of the errors he argues against have retained their currency as prepackaged sayings, though some have not (perhaps he was successful in eradicating them?). In any case, his calmly reasoned counter-arguments tend to resonate with our own "common sense."

Here is a list of the truisms he tackled:

That a Bully Is Always a Coward

That Ill-Gotten Gain Never Prospers

That a Man Must Not Laugh at His Own Jest

That Such a One Shows His Breeding—That It Is Easy
to Perceive He Is No Gentleman

That the Poor Copy the Vices of the Rich

That Enough Is as Good as a Feast

Of Two Disputants, the Warmest Is Generally in the Wrong

That Verbal Allusions Are Not Wit, Because They Will Not
Bear a Translation

That the Worst Puns Are the Best

That Handsome Is that Handsome Does

That We Must Not Look a Gift-Horse in the Mouth

That Home Is Home Though It Is Never So Homely

That You Must Love Me, and Love My Dog

That We Should Rise with the Lark

That We Should Lie Down with the Lamb

That a Sulky Temper Is a Misfortune

That a Deformed Person Is a Lord

And here's one of his counter-arguments, reprinted in its entirety:

That Ill-Gotten Gain Never Prospers

The weakest part of mankind have this saying commonest
in their mouth. It is the trite consolation administered to the
easy dupe, when he has been tricked out of his money or
estate, that the acquisition of it will do the owner no good.
But the rogues of this world—the prudenter part of them, at
least—know better; and, if the observation had been as true as
it is old, would not have failed by this time to have discovered
it. They have pretty sharp distinctions of the fluctuating and
the permanent. "Lightly come, lightly go," is a proverb, which
they can very well afford to leave, when they leave little else,
to the losers. They do not always find manors, got by rapine
or chicanery, insensibly to melt away, as the poets will have it

or that all gold glides, like thawing snow, from the thief's hand that grasps it. Church land, alienated to lay uses, was formerly denounced to have this slippery quality. But some portions of it somehow always stuck so fast, that the denunciators have been vain to postpone the prophecy of refundment to a late posterity.

Your assignment is to write your own brief contrary essay arguing against a "popular fallacy." If you haven't got one ready to complicate, here are some you might try:

Absence makes the heart grow fonder

Actions speak louder than words

The best things in life are free

The child is father of the man

The early bird catches the worm

Familiarity breeds contempt

Good fences make good neighbors

Good things come to those who wait

He who laughs last laughs best

It takes one to know one

Laughter is the best medicine

Misery loves company

The more things change, the more they stay the same

No news is good news

Seeing is believing

A soft answer turns away wrath

Two heads are better than one

If you prefer, you may want to think against the grain of some other aphorism that hasn't quite achieved the prominence of the above commonplaces. It may help to think of a pithy statement by a recognized sage (a literary figure, perhaps). If nothing immediately comes to mind, you may want to peruse *Bartlett's Familiar Quotations* or any of its equivalents online. You may also want to think of subversion not as simple contradiction, but as addition or modification. Finally, instead of limiting your writing to the general and adversarial, go ahead and write narratively, remembering an exemplary event from your life. I have done so myself recently in a series of flash essays that I call, collectively, "Contradictions."

Here's one:

A FLASH NONFICTION ESSAY

Of the Top of My Head

The other day as we left the doctor's office, my seven-year-old daughter, Adriana, brushed past me, pronouncing to the air: "I've never seen the top of my head." She kept on her way to the car, without pause, without a sidelong glance to find an answer or a response. I smiled and caught the essay she had given me.

I suspect that I *have* seen the top of my head, in a mirror or in a photograph, but I have no distinct memory of such a thing. Today, if I lean my head forward and roll my eyes upward, I can see some of the top of my head in the glass in front of me, but I can't see all of it. I wouldn't want to. Some valiant few hairs are holding on up there, but I lament their lost brothers, no matter that God has them accounted for. I count it a blessing that I am 6'5"; most people look up to instead of down on me. Atop Adriana's brother's head we find a zig-zag scar, remnant of an operation he underwent at two months to remove a prematurely fused section of his skull. Whenever he gets a haircut his teachers ask Karina and me what happened. Or they make cracks about the barber's slipping clippers.

In any case, essays such as this are best accomplished "off the top of one's head," without too much planning or proving, like the acrobatics Adriana and I perform some evenings, after *Jeopardy!*: I lie on the floor, she comes running, I grab her shoulders, kick up her legs; we twist as she flies overhead, a mess of loose hair and giggles, yet she is grace itself, from launch to landing, again and again until bedtime, when I tuck her in with a kiss on the top of her head.

Of course, I've seen the top of her head since the day she was born; this is how I first knew her. And even now, because I am nearly twice her height, when we go walking, I see the top of her head when I glance down. It is a father's perspective. Or a god's.

When Thomas Higginson asked Emily Dickinson to define poetry, she wrote, "If I feel physically as if the top of my head were taken off, I know that is poetry." Emily, I am a father. I feel that every single day.

—Patrick Madden

Jeff Gundy

WALKING, GATHERING, LISTENING
Writing from the Green World

Do you also think that beauty exists for some fabulous reason?
—Mary Oliver, "To Begin With, the Sweet Grass"

We should go forth on the shortest walk, perchance, in the spirit of undying adventure,
never to return; prepared to send back our embalmed hearts only, as relics to our desolate
kingdoms. If you are ready to leave father and mother, and brother and sister, and wife
and child and friends, and never see them again; if you have paid your debts, and made
your will, and settled all your affairs, and are a free man; then you are ready for a walk.
—Henry David Thoreau, "Walking"

What do I know about flash nonfiction? If anything, I know that it comes
to me mostly when I am trying to write a poem, and the poem slides,
slumps, or shivers into prose. Then, sometimes, the prose gradually
wriggles and bends itself into a different sort of shapeliness, one bound
to the sentence rather than to the line. Is this then flash nonfiction, or
a prose poem, or something else? I'll leave that to the experts at definition. Sometimes, too, flash nonfictions emerge when I'm thinking
of myself as a writer of nonfiction, and they always fit within that "try
something" understanding of what an essay is. And certainly, they often
fit with Thoreau's sense that writers ought to spend their time walking,
looking, adventuring into the open territories outside their own desolate kingdoms.

Jeff Gundy's eight books of poetry and prose include *A Community of Memory: My Days with George and Clara* (1996), the first volume in University of Illinois Press's Creative Nonfiction series, and *Scattering Point: The World in a Mennonite Eye* (2003). A 2008 Fulbright Lecturer at the University of Salzburg, he is working on a manuscript about that experience, currently titled *The Other Side of Empire*. Recent essays, poems, and reviews have appeared in *The Georgia Review*, *The Sun*, *Image*, *Kenyon Review*, and *Christian Century*. He is a professor of English at Bluffton University in Ohio.

To investigate these wider realms, I have come to believe a writer needs to deflect and distract the imperial ego, the sentimentally arrogant interior demon who earnestly believes that its every quaver of emotion, its every memory of a pretty girl in the lunchroom or of Cubs games on the radio as father and son build a birdhouse together, is the stuff of immortal literature. If the writer can lull the ego into bored torpor or get it to bound away to chase squirrels and sniff around in the leaves, the parts of the psyche that only unfold and stretch themselves when there are no walls around them—which mostly have to do with paying attention to the world outside the self—can get something done.

There are various strategies for this shifting of focus, but I find walking or running—going outside in general—among the most dependable. Plenty of memorable and important things happen within rooms, and much excellent prose has been written about that; I have read and written fair amounts of it myself. Yet I also find myself drawn elsewhere, as reader, writer, and teacher. The students I encounter (mainly undergrads) are understandably young and understandably prone to thinking of themselves as the centers of their earths, sinful or otherwise. They also lean, even in classes named "creative nonfiction," toward the functional and, well, prosaic language that they've been trained to produce, even when writing about their own lives. They need to be drawn toward beauty and persuaded to speculate and explore, as Mary Oliver suggests, the beautiful's fabulous reasons for being.

I'm convinced that we all are better off when reminded that there are beings and forces not made by human beings but worth our attention; that there are energies larger, older, and subtler than our little human knots. Just placing ourselves among them is worth something, especially if we aim to be the sort of writers whose work responds to more than our private personal concerns. So the sort of writing I am advocating here begins with getting out into the open.

Space won't allow the lengthy lesson/diatribe I would love to deliver on this subject; two brief advocates for my line of thinking must suffice. One is Scott Russell Sanders, who in his book *Secrets of the Universe*, insists that "writers will have to free themselves from human enclosures, and go outside to study the green world. . . . If we are to survive, we must

look outward from the charmed circle of our own works, to the stupen-
dous theatre where our tiny, brief play goes on."

Less familiar but equally compelling, ecologist/philosopher David
Abram argues in *Becoming Animal: An Earthly Cosmology* that our sense
of separation from the natural world is simply an illusion: "We are in
and of the world, materially embedded in the same rain-drenched field
that the rocks and the ravens inhabit . . . All our knowledge, in this sense,
is carnal knowledge, born of the encounter between our flesh and the
cacophonous landscape we inhabit." If this is so, then shouldn't all our
writing be embedded in the landscapes we inhabit?

Still, there are challenges. In the Northwestern Ohio climate I live in,
spending time outside means contending with snow, ice, and bluster in
the winter and bugs, humidity, and swelter in summertime. My general
sloth and enslavement to habit and technology provide further obsta-
cles. When I can, though, I defy them all for an hour or two, and sometimes even manage to make these fortunate interludes coincide with
classes and send my students off, separately or together, to walk and look
and listen.

Over the years I have devised, borrowed, and stolen various exercises
for encouraging this sort of attention and the kinds of writing that can
result. Sometimes I simply ask students to go for a walk alone, in the
natural world (always my choice) or in town (which leads to unexpected
discoveries as well).

Another good practice is the group walk[1] (the best time for this is just
at dusk). Try to convince everyone to cease the usual chatter, to walk qui-
etly, and to open themselves to whatever is happening around them—
mostly quiet and undramatic things, though sometimes there's a sunset
or a waterfall or a surprisingly grand vista. Walk for a while, somewhere
with trees and flowing water if possible, but if not, wherever there's some
space and not too many people. Stop now and then to have someone
read a brief passage or two—maybe something you've been reading in

---

[1] I learned most of what I know about this sort of activity from poet
Terry Hermsen and naturalist Nelson Strong, during a series of
"Language of Nature" workshops at the Cuyahoga Valley National Park.

class, maybe something brand new. Oliver, Thoreau, Antonio Machado, Annie Dillard; something that *sounds* resonant and beautiful in the twilight. There's no need to explain, discuss, or elaborate.

Have some destination in mind where the group can settle in just as it's starting to get truly dark. Read a little more aloud once you get there, then invite people to spread out a bit, take out their notebooks, and just see what comes. Write until it's too dark to see; there's something about scrawling on a nearly invisible page that brings out things you would never find otherwise. I have learned over and over that the world always has something to say, if we can quiet ourselves long enough to listen.

A FLASH NONFICTION EXERCISE

Here's an exercise that defines writing objectives a bit more closely than the group walk requires; if I were using it during a group walk, I would distribute and discuss it beforehand.

Walking and Gathering

Do some wandering, either in a group or by yourself. Don't be in a hurry. If you're in a group, pay attention to what's being said and done by the leaders, but don't be limited to that.

As you go, be alert for anything you can pick up: any specific elements of the surroundings, small or large, that catch your attention for any reason: because they are beautiful, strange, unexpected, uncomfortable.

Record them in your notebook.

Don't be restricted to visual images—use as many senses as possible.

Don't worry about whether these details fit together, form some sort of pattern, or will cohere into a neat story.

Writing

Write a sentence from the point of view of some animal, plant, or natural object. If you were a pond lily, a white-tailed deer, a mother skunk, a tulip tree, a lost goose feather, what would you have to say?

Beyond giving whatever you choose the consciousness needed to speak, try to avoid too much personification—keep the perceptions and voice as close as you can to the actual qualities.

When you have one sentence, step back: where to go from here? Some possibilities:

- A narrative of some sort, staying with this point of view?

- A way of spiraling deeper into the inner being of whatever you have chosen? Of expanding outward?

- Are there two points of view in some sort of conflict?

- The possibility of shifting to another, related point of view, and then another and another?

Let the piece take whatever direction seems most rewarding, and keep riding the wave until it reaches some kind of resolution. Read back over it, tinker and fiddle as needed, and be ready to share with the group (if you are with others) and receive public acclaim.

Below is a brief piece of mine, written during a group walk with one of my classes.

A FLASH NONFICTION ESSAY

From the Rocks at Dusk

I didn't expect this much light. The heavy earth had spun us away from the moon and the sun, but still the lights on their poles blazed like barren torches and every window leaked, the filaments aglow and the photons slashing everywhere, altering everything, not at all like the bat that darted and swung above us in search of the earliest mosquitos. More like the wailing from the highway, each minivan and semi reduced by speed and distance to an abstract moan.

I wanted to walk back into the woods, pull them up around me like a hooded sweatshirt, and how vain was that? Every tree has its story but none of them were testifying, with immunity or without. Nothing is lost but some things are broken, some are splintered, some must wait longer than fossils for regeneration or a good cool drink.

While my eyes were adjusting I remembered the difference between desire and need. I recalled just what my will means to the world at large. Then I tried bargaining, and pretending not to care, and blinking and glancing sideways. I would tell you what finally worked, if anything had worked. I have about as much patience as a gnat. There weren't any gnats.

I kept pushing the pen across paper, breathed twice slowly, straightened my back. The wet dirt was still cold with winter, its small lives just stirring. Some odd phrases slipped through me like eels. Water muttered on down the creek, bending to geography, obeying the urge to settle. In the great darkness there were many small lights, and as every one of us fell deeper into evening I found myself believing that the darkness itself was on fire.

—Jeff Gundy, from *Spoken among the Trees*

FURTHER READING

The contributors, editor, and press recommend the following:

ANTHOLOGIES

In Brief: Short Takes on the Personal. Eds. Judith Kitchen and Mary Paumier Jones. New York: Norton, 1995.

In Short: A Collection of Brief Creative Nonfiction. Eds. Judith Kitchen and Mary Paumier Jones. New York: Norton, 1996.

Short Takes: Brief Encounters with Contemporary Nonfiction. Ed. Judith Kitchen. New York: Norton, 2005.

SINGLE-AUTHOR COLLECTIONS

Adorno, Theodor. *Minima Moralia*. New York: Verso, 1974.

Cantú, Norma Elia. *Canicula: Snapshots of a Girlhood en la Frontera*. Albuquerque: University of New Mexico Press, 1997.

Cappello, Mary. *Awkward: A Detour*. New York: Bellevue Literary Press, 2007.

Cooper, Bernard. *Maps to Anywhere*. Athens, GA: University of Georgia Press, 1997.

Cooper, Bernard. *Truth Serum: A Memoir*. New York: Houghton Mifflin, 1996.

Doyle Brian. *Leaping: Revelations and Epiphanies*. Chicago: Loyola University Press, 2003.

Fénéon, Félix. *Novels in Three Lines*. Trans. Luc Sante. New York: New York Review Books, 2007.

Galeano, Eduardo. *Genesis: Memory of Fire Trilogy*. New York: Norton, 1998.

Galeano, Eduardo. *The Book of Embraces*. New York: Norton, 1999.

Gombrowicz, Witold. *Diary*. Chicago: Northwestern University Press, 1988.

Guess, Carol. *My Father in Water*. Exeter, UK: Shearsman, 2011.

Holm, Bill. *Coming Home Crazy: An Alphabet of China Essays*. Minneapolis: Milkweed Editions, 1990.

Hurd, Barbara. *Walking the Wrack Line: On Tidal Shifts and What Remains*. Athens, GA: University of Georgia Press, 2008.

Kitchen, Judith. *Distance and Direction*. Minneapolis: Coffee House, 2001.

Lennon, J. Robert. *Pieces for the Left Hand*. London: Granta, 2005.

Nelson, Maggie. *Bluets*. Seattle: Wave Books, 2009.

Nietzsche, Friedrich. *The Gay Science*. New York: Vintage, 1974.

Norris, Kathleen. *Dakota: A Spiritual Geography*. New York: Houghton Mifflin, 2001.

O'Connor, Flannery. *Habits of Being: Letters of Flannery O'Connor*. Ed. Sally Fitzgerald. New York: Farrar, Straus, and Giroux, 1988.

Purpura, Lia. *Increase*. Athens, GA: University of Georgia Press, 2000.

Purpura, Lia. *On Looking: Essays*. Louisville, KY: Sarabande Books, 2006.

Shōnagan, Sei. *The Pillow Book*. Trans. Meredith McKinney. New York: Penguin, 2006.

Shumaker, Peggy. *Just Breathe Normally*. Lincoln, NE: University of Nebraska Press, 2007.

Sutin, Lawrence. *A Postcard Memoir*. Saint Paul, Minnesota: Graywolf Press, 2000.

Thomas, Abigail. *Safekeeping: Some True Stories from a Life*. New York: Knopf, 2000.

Weil, Simone. *Gravity and Grace*. New York: Routledge, 1952.

Winik, Marion. *Glen Rock Book of the Dead*. Berkeley, CA: Counterpoint, 2010.

Yuknavitch, Lidia. *The Chronology of Water: A Memoir*. Portland, OR: Hawthorne Books, 2011.

INDIVIDUAL ESSAYS

Alexie, Sherman. "Somebody Else's Genocide." *Brevity* 31 (2009). Web.

Allison, Sue. "Not the Great Books." *Fourth Genre: Explorations in Nonfiction* 6:1 (2004). Print.

Beard, Jo Ann. "Preface." *The Boys of My Youth*. New York: Little, Brown, 1998.

Birkerts, Sven. "The Finger Writes." *Water~Stone Review* 11 (2008). Print.

Borges, Jorge Luis. "Borges and I." *Who's Writing This? Notations on the Authorial I with Self-Portraits*. Ed. Daniel Halpern. New York: Harper Perennial, 2009.

Chernoff, Maxine. "Her Many Occupations." *Seneca Review* 30:1 (2000). Print.

Cooper, Bernard. "Where to Begin." *Truth Serum: A Memoir*. New York: Houghton Mifflin, 1996.

Heaney, Seamus. "Subject + Object." *Granta* 102 (2008). Print.

Kitchen, Judith. "On the Farm." *Brevity* 27 (2008). Web.

Lamb, Charles. "Popular Fallacies." *The Complete Works and Letters of Charles and Mary Lamb*. New York: Modern Library, 1935.

Maso, Carol. "Richter, the Enigma." *Seneca Review* 30:1 (2000). Print.

McClanahan, Rebecca. "Loving Bald Men." *Brevity* 12 (2002). Web.

Miller, Brenda. "Split." *Brevity* 11 (2002). Web.

Moore, Dinty W. "Mr. Plimpton's Revenge." http://tinyurl.com/plimptonmap

Neal, Harmony. "White on White." *Prick of the Spindle* 1:1 (2007). Web.

Olson, Christina. "Duck, North Carolina." *Brevity* 30 (2009). Web.

Ondaatje, Michael. "Photograph." *Running in the Family*. New York: Vintage, 1993.

Panning, Anne. "Candy Cigarettes." *Brevity* 23 (2007). Web.

Peckham, Rachael. "The Origin of Sausage." *Brevity* 22 (2006). Web.

Prewitt, Ellen Morris. "Tetanus, You Understand?" *Brevity* 14 (2003). Web.

Root Jr., Robert L. "Collage, Montage, Mosaic, Vignette, Episode, Segment." *The Fourth Genre: Contemporary Writers of/on Creative Nonfiction*. New York: Pearson Longman, 2007.

Shihab Nye, Naomi. "Someone I Love." *Short Takes: Brief Encounters with Contemporary Nonfiction*. Ed. Judith Kitchen. New York: Norton, 2005.

Simic, Charles. "Three Fragments." *In Short: A Collection of Brief Creative Nonfiction*. Eds. Judith Kitchen and Mary Paumier Jones. New York: Norton, 1996.

Updike, David. "Drinking, Driving and Paying." *The New York Times Magazine* 5 Dec. 2010.

Wadsworth, Sarah. "Too Slow for Your Speed." *Flashquake* 9:4 (2010). Web.

Wenderoth, Joe. "Things to Do Today." *Seneca Review* 30:1 (2000). Print.

Wiggins, Alexis. "My Mother's Touch." *Brevity* 18 (2005). Web.

Woolf, Virginia. "The Death of the Moth." *The Death of the Moth and Other Essays*. New York: Harcourt, 1942.

CREDITS

Susanne Antonetta: "Little Things" first appeared in *Brevity* (brevitymag.com). Reprinted by permission of the author.

Barrie Jean Borich: "Dogged" first appeared in *Sweet: A Literary Confection*. Reprinted by permission of the author.

Jenny Boully: "Strange Mechanism for a Dream" first appeared in *The Book of Beginnings and Endings* by Jenny Boully, Sarabande Books, 2007. Reprinted by permission of the author.

Jimmy Chen: "The Water Is Rising Pleas" first appeared in *Brevity* (brevitymag.com). Reprinted by permission of the author.

Brian Doyle: "Leap" first appeared in *The American Scholar*. Reprinted by permission of the author.

Rigoberto González: "Toy Soldier" from *Autobiography of My Hunger*, forthcoming from University of Wisconsin Press, 2013. Reprinted by permission of the author.

Carol Guess: "Of Carnival Lights, Compression, and Mice"' first appeared in *My Father in Water* by Carol Guess, Shearsman Books, 2011. Reprinted by permission of Shearsman Books.

Jeff Gundy: "From the Rocks at Dusk" first appeared in *Spoken Among the Trees* by Jeff Gundy, University of Akron Press, 2007. Reprinted by permission of the author.

Robin Hemley: "Twirl/Run" first appeared in *Drunken Boat* and in *Twirl/Run,* powerHouse Books, 2009. Reprinted by permission of the author.

Dinah Lenney: "Little Black Dress" first appeared in *Chaparral* (www.chaparralpoetry.net). Reprinted by permission of the author.

Patrick Madden: "Of the Top of My Head" first appeared in *Superstition Review* (as part of "Contradictions"). Reprinted by permission of the author.

Debra Marquart: "Hochzeit" first appeared in *Brevity* (brevitymag.com) and in *The Horizontal World: Growing Up Wild in the Middle of Nowhere* by Debra Marquart, Counterpoint, 2006. Reprinted by permission of the author.

Lee Martin: "Dumber Than" first appeared in *Brevity* (brevitymag.com). Reprinted by permission of the author.

Maggie McKnight: "France 1993" first appeared in *Backwards City Review*. Reprinted by permission of the author.

Brenda Miller: "Friendship, Intuition, and Trust: On the Importance of Detail" first appeared in a slightly different version on the *Brevity* blog and "Swerve" first appeared in *Brevity* (brevitymag.com). Both reprinted by permission of the author.

Aimee Nezhukumatathil: "The Soils I Have Eaten" first appeared in *Brevity* (brevity-mag.com). Reprinted by permission of the author.

Anne Panning: "The White Suit" first appeared in *River Teeth*. Reprinted by permission of the author.

Lia Purpura: "On Miniatures" first appeared in *Brevity* (brevitymag.com). Reprinted by permission of the author. "Augury" first appeared in *On Looking: Essays* by Lia Purpura, Sarabande Books, 2006. Reprinted by permission of Sarabande Books, www.sarabandebooks.org.

Sheryl St. Germain: "What We're Good At" first appeared in *Brevity* (brevitymag.com). Reprinted by permission of the author.

Peggy Shumaker: "Moving Water, Tucson" first appeared in *Short Takes: Brief Encounters with Contemporary Nonfiction*, W. W. Norton, 2005. Reprinted by permission of the author.

Sue William Silverman: "Archipelago" first appeared in *Brevity* (brevitymag.com). Reprinted by permission of the author.

Ira Sukrungruang: "What If?" first appeared in *Brevity* (brevitymag.com). Reprinted by permission of the author.

Nicole Walker: "Dissociation (The Natural Order)" first appeared in *Agni Online*. Reprinted by permission of the author.

ACKNOWLEDGMENTS

In addition to the sources fully cited in the introduction, the following sources were referenced:

Fakundiny, Lydia. *The Art of the Essay*. Boston: Houghton Mifflin, 1991.

Gracia, Jynelle. "Right into the Fire: Notes on the Nonfiction Short: An Interview with Judith Kitchen and Dinty W. Moore." *River Teeth: A Journal of Nonfiction Narrative*, Volume 8, Number 1, Fall 2006, pp. 123–135.

Klaus, Carl, and Ned Stuckey-French, eds. *Essayists on the Essay: Four Centuries of Commentary*. Iowa City: University of Iowa Press, 2011.

Lopate, Phillip, ed. *The Art of the Personal Essay: An Anthology from the Classical Era to the Present*. New York: Anchor-Doubleday, 1994.

Stuckey-French, Ned. *The American Essay in the American Century*. Columbia: University of Missouri Press, 2011.

Kitchen, Judith, and Mary Paumier Jones, eds. *In Brief: Short Takes on the Personal*. New York: Norton, 1995.

First and foremost, the authors, editors, and teachers who shared their ideas, exercises, prompts, and example essays in this *Field Guide* must be thanked, thanked again, given a very deep bow, and offered an enthusiastic round of applause. They are a generous, brilliant, and inspired group of artists, and there would, of course, be no book without them.

I want to offer my sincere gratitude as well to my two extraordinary editors, Kathleen Rooney and Abigail Beckel, founders of Rose Metal Press and true champions of the flash form.

Thanks as well to Ned Stuckey-French, Eric LeMay, Patrick Madden, Sarah Einstein, and Joey Franklin for advice and encouragement, and to Renita Romasco and Maria Romasco Moore for ongoing support.

I am, indeed, indebted to all of the authors, volunteer editors, and readers of *Brevity* over the years. The flash nonfiction form exists and thrives thanks to these thousands of devoted individuals.

Finally, my sincerest thanks to Judith Kitchen, for first introducing me to the flash nonfiction form, for encouraging me in my own exploration, and for always being a warm-hearted, bright-smiling mentor and friend.

ABOUT THE EDITOR

Dinty W. Moore is the author of the memoir *Between Panic & Desire*, winner of the Grub Street Nonfiction Book Prize in 2009. His other books include *The Accidental Buddhist, Toothpick Men, The Emperor's Virtual Clothes*, and the writing guides *The Mindful Writer: Noble Truths of the Writing Life* and *Crafting the Personal Essay: A Guide for Writing and Publishing Creative Nonfiction*. Moore has published essays and stories in *The Southern Review, The Georgia Review, Harper's, The New York Times Sunday Magazine, The Philadelphia Inquirer, Gettysburg Review, Utne Reader*, and *Crazyhorse*, among numerous other venues. A professor of nonfiction writing at Ohio University, Moore has won many awards for his writing, including a National Endowment for the Arts Fellowship in Fiction. He edits *Brevity*, an online journal of flash nonfiction, and serves on the editorial boards of *Creative Nonfiction* and *New Ohio Review*. He regularly teaches workshops across the country and in Europe and currently lives in Athens, Ohio, where he grows heirloom tomatoes and edible dandelions.